GREAT TASTES

LITTLE CAKES

First published in 2009 by Bay Books, an imprint of Murdoch Books Pty Limited
This edition published in 2010.

Murdoch Books Australia
Pier 8/9
23 Hickson Road
Millers Point NSW 2000
Phone: +61 (0) 2 8220 2000
Fax: +61 (0) 2 8220 2558
www.murdochbooks.com.au

Murdoch Books UK Limited
Erico House, 6th Floor
93–99 Upper Richmond Road
Putney, London SW15 2TG
Phone: +44 (0) 20 8785 5995
Fax: +44 (0) 20 8785 5985
www.murdochbooks.co.uk

Chief Executive: Juliet Rogers
Publishing Director: Kay Scarlett
Publisher: Lynn Lewis
Senior Designer: Heather Menzies
Designer: Wendy Inkster
Production: Kita George
Index: Jo Rudd

ISBN: 9781741968668

PRINTED IN CHINA

IMPORTANT: Those who might be at risk from the effects of salmonella poisoning (the elderly, pregnant women, young children and those suffering from immune deficiency diseases) should consult their doctor with any concerns about eating raw eggs.

OVEN GUIDE: You may find cooking times vary depending on the oven you are using. For fan-forced ovens, as a general rule, set the oven temperature to 20°C (35°F) lower than indicated in the recipe.

GREAT TASTES

LITTLE CAKES

More than 120 easy recipes for every day

bay books

CONTENTS

ANYTIME CAKES

CHOCOLATE HAZELNUT FRIANDS

MAKES 12

200 g (7 oz) whole hazelnuts

185 g (6½ oz) unsalted butter

6 egg whites

155 g (5½ oz/1¼ cups) plain
(all-purpose) flour

30 g (1 oz/¼ cup) cocoa powder

250 g (9 oz/2 cups) icing
(confectioners') sugar

icing (confectioners') sugar, extra,
to dust

1 **Preheat the oven** to 200°C (400°F/Gas 6). Lightly grease twelve ½-cup (125 ml/4 fl oz) friand or muffin tins. Spread the hazelnuts out on a baking tray. Bake for 8–10 minutes, or until fragrant, taking care not to burn the hazelnuts. Place in a clean tea towel (dish towel) and rub vigorously to loosen the skins. Cool, then process in a food processor until finely ground.

2 **Place the butter** in a small pan and melt over medium heat, then cook for 3–4 minutes, or until butter turns a deep golden colour. Strain any dark solids and set aside to cool (the colour will become deeper on standing).

3 **Lightly whisk the egg** whites in a bowl until frothy but not firm. Sift the flour, cocoa powder and icing sugar into a large mixing bowl and stir in the ground hazelnuts. Make a well in the centre and add the egg whites and butter and mix until combined.

4 **Spoon the mixture** into the prepared tins until three-quarters filled. Bake for 20–25 minutes, or until a skewer inserted into the centre comes out clean. Leave in the tin for a few minutes, then turn out onto a wire rack to cool completely. Dust with icing sugar, to serve.

PETITS FOURS

MAKES 16

1 egg

2 tablespoons caster sugar

40 g (1½ oz/⅓ cup) plain flour

15 g (½ oz) butter, melted

ICING (FROSTING)

150 g (5 oz/½ cup) apricot jam, warmed and strained

2 teaspoons liqueur

120 g (4 oz) marzipan

200 g (8 oz) soft icing (frosting), ready-made

1 tablespoon water

1 **Preheat the oven** to 180°C. Brush a 26 x 8 x 4.5 cm bar tin with melted butter or oil. Line the base and sides with baking paper.

2 **Using electric beaters,** beat the egg and sugar in a medium bowl for 5 minutes until very thick and pale. Fold in the sifted flour and melted butter quickly and lightly, using a metal spoon.

3 **Pour the mixture** into prepared tin and bake for 15 minutes, or until lightly golden and springy to the touch. Leave in the tin for 3 minutes before turning out onto a wire rack to cool.

4 **Using a 3 cm round cutter,** cut out rounds from the cake. Brush the top and sides of each with combined jam and liqueur. Roll the marzipan out to a thickness of 2 mm, cut out rounds and strips to cover the top and sides of the cakes.

5 **Place the icing** and water in a heatproof bowl and stand over a pan of simmering water. Stir until the icing has melted and the mixture is smooth.

6 **Place the marzipan-covered cakes** onto a wire rack over a tray. Spoon the icing over each cake and use a flat-bladed knife to spread evenly over the base and sides. Reheat the icing over the pan if it begins to thicken.

7 **Leave the cakes** to set. Carefully lift the cakes from the rack and place each one in a paper petit four case, decorate with small purchased coloured fondant flowers if desired.

Note: Petits fours will keep for up to 2 days in an airtight container in a cool, dark place. Place in a single layer in container.

JAM-FILLED DONUTS

MAKES 14

185 ml (6 fl oz/¾ cup) lukewarm milk

1 tablespoon dried yeast

2 tablespoons caster (superfine) sugar

310 g (11 oz/2½ cups) plain
(all-purpose) flour

2 teaspoons ground cinnamon

1 teaspoon finely grated lemon zest

2 eggs, separated

40 g (1½ oz) unsalted butter, softened

105 g (3¾ oz/⅓ cup) plum, strawberry or
apricot jam

oil, for deep-frying

caster (superfine) sugar, extra, for rolling

1 Put the milk in a small bowl, add the yeast and
1 tablespoon of the sugar. Leave in a warm, draught-free place
for 10 minutes, or until bubbles appear on the surface. The
mixture should be frothy and slightly increased in volume. If
your yeast doesn't foam, it is dead, so you will have to discard
it and start again.

2 Sift the flour into a large bowl and add the cinnamon,
lemon zest, egg yolks, yeast mixture, remaining sugar, and
a pinch of salt. Mix well, then place the dough on a lightly
floured work surface and knead for 5 minutes. Work in the
butter, a little at a time, continually kneading until the dough
becomes elastic. This should take about 10 minutes. Place
in a large bowl and cover with a clean, damp tea towel (dish
towel). Leave to rise overnight in the refrigerator.

3 Place the dough on a lightly floured work surface and roll
out to 3 mm (⅛ inch) thick. Using a 6 cm (2½ inch) cutter, cut
28 rounds from the dough. Place 14 of the rounds on a lightly
floured tray and carefully place ¾ teaspoon of the jam into the
centre of each. Lightly beat the egg whites, then brush around
the outside edges of the rounds, being careful not to touch the
jam at all. Top with the remaining 14 rounds and press down
firmly around the edges to seal. Cover with a clean tea towel
(leave to rise for 30 minutes. Make sure the dough has not
separated at the edges. Press open edges firmly together.

4 Fill a deep-fryer or large heavy-based saucepan one-
third full of oil and heat to 170°C (325°F), or until a cube of
bread dropped into the oil browns in 20 seconds. Cook the
doughnuts in batches for 1½ minutes on both sides, or until
golden. Drain, then roll in the extra sugar. Serve immediately.

INDIVIDUAL CHEESECAKES WITH MACERATED STRAWBERRIES

SERVES 4

90 g (3¼ oz/¾ cup) sweet biscuit (cookie) crumbs

90 g (3¼ oz/1 cup) toasted flaked almonds, lightly crushed

100g (3½ oz/⅔ cup) white chocolate chopped, melted

60 g (2¼ oz/¼ cup) unsalted butter, melted

FILLING

2 teaspoons powdered gelatine

250 g (9 oz/1 cup) softened cream cheese

80 g (2¾ oz/⅓ cup) caster (superfine) sugar

1 teaspoon finely grated orange zest

2 tablespoons orange juice

125 ml (4 fl oz/½ cup) pouring cream

1 egg white, at room temperature

MACERATED STRAWBERRIES

500 g (1 lb 2 oz/3⅓ cups) strawberries, hulled

1 tablespoon caster (superfine) sugar

¼ teaspoon finely grated orange zest

2 tablespoons orange juice

1 **Lightly grease** a 12–hole standard muffin pan. Line each hole with two long strips of baking paper in the shape of a cross to help remove the cheesecakes.

2 **Put the biscuit crumbs,** almonds, white chocolate, and butter in a bowl and stir until just combined, adding more butter if the mixture is too dry. Divide the mixture among the muffin holes and use your fingers to press it over the bases and up the sides, smoothing with the back of a spoon. Refrigerate the crusts while preparing the filling.

3 **To make the filling,** put 1 tablespoon (20 ml) of water in a small bowl and sprinkle with the gelatin. Leave the gelatin to sponge and swell.

4 **Beat the cream cheese,** sugar and orange zest in a small bowl with an electric beater until light and creamy. Beat in the orange juice until combined. Stir in the gelatin mixture until combined and creamy. (Warm the gelatine mixture slightly if it has become too spongy.)

5 **Whip the cream** until soft peaks form. In a separate bowl, whisk the egg white with a clean whisk until soft peaks form. Fold the cream and egg white into the cream-cheese mixture. Spoon into the prepared crusts and refrigerate for several hours, overnight or until set.

6 **To make the macerated strawberries,** cut strawberries into small pieces. Combine the strawberries with the sugar, orange zest and orange juice and refrigerate for several hours.

7 **To serve,** carefully remove the cheesecakes from the muffin pan and top with a spoonful of strawberries.

BABY COFFEE AND WALNUT SOUR CREAM CAKES

MAKES 24

75 g (2½ oz/¾ cup) walnuts

155 g (5½ oz/⅔ cup) firmly packed soft brown sugar

125 g (4½ oz) unsalted butter, softened

2 eggs, lightly beaten

125 g (4½ oz/1 cup) self-raising flour

80 g (3 oz/⅓ cup) sour cream

1 tablespoon strong black coffee

1 **Preheat the oven** to 160°C (315°F/ Gas 2–3). Lightly grease two 12-hole 60 ml (2 fl oz/¼ cup) baby muffin tins. Process the walnuts and 45 g (1½ oz/ ¼ cup) of the brown sugar in a food processor until the walnuts are roughly chopped into small pieces. Transfer to a mixing bowl.

2 **Cream the butter** and remaining sugar together in the food processor until pale and creamy. With the motor running, gradually add the egg and process until smooth. Add the flour and blend until well mixed. Add the sour cream and coffee and process until thoroughly mixed.

3 **Spoon ½ teaspoon** of the walnut and sugar mixture into the base of each muffin hole, followed by a teaspoon of the cake mixture. Sprinkle a little more walnut mixture over the top, a little more cake mixture and top with the remaining walnut mixture.

4 **Bake for 20 minutes,** or until risen and springy to the touch. Leave in the tins for 5 minutes. Remove the cakes using a flat-bladed knife to loosen the side and base, then transfer to a wire rack to cool completely.

SPONGE FINGERS

MAKES 24

80 g (3 oz/⅓ cup) self-raising flour

2 tablespoons cornflour

2 eggs, seperated

80 g (3 oz/⅓ cup) caster (superfine) sugar

20 g (¾ oz) unsalted butter, melted

160 ml (5 fl oz/⅔ cup) cream

½ teaspoon imitation vanilla essence

icing (confectioners') sugar, for dusting

1   **Preheat the oven** to 180°C (350°F/Gas 4). Brush two 32 x 38 cm biscuit trays with melted butter or oil, line the bases with grease paper. Dust the tins lightly with flour and shake off the excess. Mark lines in the flour 7 cm apart on each tray.

2   **Sift the flours** three times onto greaseproof paper.

3   **Place the egg whites** in a small mixing bowl. Using electric beaters, beat until firm peaks form. Add the sugar gradually, beating constantly until dissolved and the mixture is glossy and thick.

4   **Add the beaten egg yolks,** beat a further 20 seconds.

5   **Transfer the mixture** to a large mixing bowl. Using a metal spoon fold in the flours gradually and lightly. Add the butter and fold through.

6   **Place the mixture** in a large piping bag fitted with a round nozzle. Pipe fingers between the 7 cm lines, leaving 5 cm between each one.

7   **Bake for 6 minutes** or until lightly golden. Leave the sponge fingers on the tins for 5 minutes before placing them on a wire rack to cool. Beat the cream and vanilla essence in a small bowl until stiff peaks form.

8   **To assemble,** sandwich two sponge fingers together with a spoonful of whipped cream. Dust with sifted icing sugar just before serving.

Note: Filled fingers are best eaten immediately. For a variation spoon the mixture into rounds and fold a few finely chopped strawberries through the whipped cream, if desired.

PISTACHIO FRIENDS

MAKES 10

165 g (5¾ oz/1⅓ cups) icing (confectioners') sugar, plus extra for dusting

40 g (1½ oz/⅓ cup) plain (all-purpose) flour

125 g (4½ oz/1 cup) ground pistachio nuts

160 g (5¾ oz) unsalted butter, melted

5 egg whites, lightly beaten

½ teaspoon natural vanilla extract

55 g (2 oz/¼ cup) caster (superfine) sugar

35 g (1¼ oz/¼ cup) chopped pistachio nuts

1 **Preheat the oven** to 190°C (375°F/Gas 5). Lightly grease ten 125 ml (4 fl oz/½ cup) friand tins.

2 **Sift the icing sugar** and flour into a bowl. Add the ground pistachios, butter, egg whites and vanilla and stir with a metal spoon until just combined.

3 **Spoon the mixture** into the prepared tins, place on a baking tray and bake for 15–20 minutes, or until a skewer inserted into the centre of a friand comes out clean. Leave in the tins for 5 minutes, then turn out onto a wire rack to cool.

4 **Meanwhile,** put the sugar and 60 ml (2 fl oz/¼ cup) water in a small saucepan and stir over low heat until the sugar has dissolved. Increase the heat, then boil for 4 minutes, or until thick and syrupy. Remove from the heat and stir in the chopped pistachios, then, working quickly, spoon the mixture over the tops of the friands. Dust with icing sugar and serve.

Note: Friends will keep, stored in an airtight container, for up to 4 days, or frozen for up to 3 months.

INDIVIDUAL STICKY DATE CAKES

MAKES 6

270 g (9½ oz/1½ cups) stoned dates, chopped

1 teaspoon bicarbonate of soda (baking soda)

150 g (5 oz) unsalted butter, chopped

185 g (6 oz/1½ cups) self-raising flour

265 g (9½ oz) firmly packed soft brown sugar

2 eggs, lightly beaten

2 tablespoons golden syrup (dark corn syrup)

185 ml (6 fl oz) cream

1   Preheat the oven to 180°C (350°F/Gas 4). Grease six 1-cup (250 ml/9 fl oz) muffin holes. Place the dates and 1 cup (250 ml/9 fl oz) water in a saucepan, bring to the boil. Remove from the heat and stir in the bicarbonate of soda. Add 60 g (2 oz) of the butter and stir until dissolved.

2   Sift flour into a large bowl, add 125 g (4½ oz/2/3 cup) sugar and stir. Make a well in the centre, add the date mixture and egg and stir until just combined. Spoon the mixture evenly into the prepared muffin tin and bake for about 20 minutes, or until a skewer comes out clean when inserted in the centre of a muffin.

3   To make the sauce, place the golden syrup and cream with the remaining butter and sugar in a small saucepan and stir over low heat for 3–4 minutes, or until the sugar has dissolved. Bring to the boil, then reduce the heat and simmer, stirring the sauce occasionally, for 2 minutes. To serve, turn the cakes out onto serving plates, pierce the tops a few times with a skewer and drizzle with the sauce.

VANILLA AND CREAM CHEESE CAKES

MAKES 12

60g (2¼ oz) unsalted butter, softened

115 g (4 oz/½ cup) caster (superfine) sugar

1 teaspoon finely grated lemon zest

1 egg

1 egg yolk

60 g (2¼ oz/½ cup) plain (all-purpose) flour

1 tablespoon self-raising flour

2 tablespoons sour cream

CHEESECAKE TOPPING

250 g (9 oz) cream cheese, softened

115 g (4 oz/½ cup) caster (superfine) sugar

2 eggs

160 g (5¾ oz/⅔ cup) sour cream

1 vanilla bean or 1 teaspoon natural vanilla extract

2 tablespoons pine nuts

1   Preheat the oven to 180°C (350°F/Gas 4). Lightly grease twelve 125 ml (4 fl oz/½ cup) friand tins and line the bases with baking paper. Dust the sides of the tins with a little flour, shaking off any excess.

2   Cream the butter, sugar and zest in a bowl using electric beaters until pale and fluffy. Add the egg, then the egg yolk, beating well after each addition. Sift the flours into a bowl, then gently stir into the butter mixture alternately with the sour cream.

3   Divide the mixture between the friand tins. Bake for 10 minutes, or until a skewer inserted into the centre of a cake comes out clean. Remove from the oven and allow to cool. Reduce the oven to 160°C (315°F/Gas 2-3).

4   To make the cheesecake topping, beat the cream cheese and sugar in a small bowl until combined and creamy. Add the eggs one at a time, beating well after each addition, then beat in the sour cream. If using the vanilla bean, split it down the middle and scrape out the seeds. Add the seeds (or vanilla extract) to the cheese mixture, mixing well. Spoon the topping evenly over the cooled cakes and sprinkle with the pine nuts.

5   Bake for a further 12 minutes or until set. Remove from the oven and allow to cool.

COCONUT MACAROONS

MAKES 45

3 egg whites

250 g (9 oz/1 cup) caster (superfine) sugar

½ teaspoon coconut essence

1 teaspoon grated lemon zest

2 tablespoons cornflour (cornstarch), sifted

180 g (6 oz/2 cups) desiccated coconut

1 **Preheat the oven** to 180°C (350°F/Gas 4). Line two baking trays with baking paper.

2 **Place the egg whites** in a small dry mixing bowl. Using electric beaters, beat the egg whites until firm peaks form. Add the sugar gradually, beating constantly until the mixture is thick and glossy and all the sugar is dissolved. Add the coconut essence and lemon zest and beat until just combined.

3 **Transfer the mixture** to a large mixing bowl and add the cornflour and coconut. Using a metal spoon, stir until just combined.

4 **Drop 2 level teaspoons** of mixture onto the prepared trays about 3 cm (1¼ inch) apart. Bake on the top shelf of the oven for 15–20 minutes, or until golden.

5 **Leave the macaroons** to cool completely on the trays.

Note: Store in an airtight container for up to 2 days. You can sprinkle macaroons with shredded coconut before baking, if liked, and drizzle with melted chocolate before serving.

SAND CAKES WITH PASSIONFRUIT CREAM CHEESE ICING

MAKES 6

185 g (6½ oz) unsalted butter, softened

2 teaspoons natural vanilla extract

250 g (9 oz/1 cup) caster (superfine) sugar

3 eggs

185 g (6½ oz/1½ cups) self-raising flour

60 g (2¼ oz/⅓ cup) rice flour

4 tablespoons milk

PASSIONFRUIT CREAM CHEESE ICING (FROSTING)

100 g (3½ oz) cream cheese, at room temperature

90 g (3¼ oz/¾ cup) icing (confectioners') sugar, sifted

1-2 tablespoons passionfruit pulp

1 Preheat the oven to 180°C (350°F/ Gas 4). Lightly grease six standard muffin holes and line the bases with baking paper.

2 Beat the butter, vanilla extract, sugar, eggs, flours and milk using electric beaters on low speed until combined, then beat on medium speed for 3 minutes, or until thick and creamy.

3 Pour the mixture into the prepared tin and smooth the surface.

4 Bake for 20-25 minutes, or until lightly golden. Leave in the tin for 10 minutes, then turn out onto a wire rack to cool completely.

5 To make the icing (frosting), beat the cream cheese and icing sugar in a small bowl using electric beaters until light and creamy. Add the passionfruit pulp. Beat for 2 minutes, or until smooth and fluffy. Spoon over the cakes.

CHOCOLATE ALMOND TARTS

MAKES 18

125 g (4½ oz/1 cup) plain
(all-purpose) flour

pinch salt

60 g (2½ oz) unsalted butter, chopped

1 tablespoon icing (confectioners') sugar

1 tablespoon lemon juice

FILLING

1 egg

90 g (3¼ oz/½ cup) caster (superfine)
sugar

2 tablespoons cocoa powder

90 g (3¼ oz/½ cup) ground almonds

3 tablespoons thick (double/heavy)
cream

80 g (2¾ oz/¼ cup) apricot jam

18 blanched almonds

1 **Preheat the oven** to 180°C (350°F/ Gas 4). Lightly grease two flat-bottomed 9-hole cupcake trays. Process the flour, salt, butter and icing sugar in a food processor for 10 seconds, or until the mixture resembles fine breadcrumbs. Add the lemon juice and process until the mixture forms a ball. Roll between sheets of baking paper to 5 mm (¼ inch) thickness. Cut into 7 cm (2¾ inch) rounds with fluted cutter. Place in the prepared tins and chill for 20 minutes.

2 **To make the filling,** place the egg and sugar in a mixing bowl. Using electric beaters, beat until thick and pale. Sift the cocoa on top. Stir in the ground almonds and cream with a flat-bladed knife.

3 **Place a dab of jam** in each tart. Spoon the filling in and place an almond in the centre. Bake for 15 minutes, or until the top is puffed and set. Leave in the tins for 5 minutes, then turn out onto wire racks to cool.

PINK GRAPEFRUIT MERINGUE TARTLETS

MAKES 8

450 g (1 lb) ready-made sweet
   shortcrust pastry

GRAPEFRUIT CURD

100 g (3½ oz) unsalted butter, chopped

6 eggs, lightly beaten

250 ml (9 fl oz/1 cup) ruby
   grapefruit juice

1 tablespoon finely grated ruby
   grapefruit zest

170 g (6 oz/¾ cup) caster
   (superfine) sugar

MERINGUE

4 egg whites, at room temperature

115 g (4 oz/½ cup) caster
   (superfine) sugar

1 tablespoon cornflour (cornstarch)

icing sugar, to dust

grated lemon zest, to garnish

1 **Preheat the oven** to 180°C (350°F/Gas 4). Lightly grease eight loose-based tartlet tins, 10 cm (4 inches) in diameter and 3 cm (1¼ inches) deep.

2 **Roll out the pastry** on a lightly floured work surface to 3 mm (⅛ inch) thick. Cut the pastry into rounds to fit the base and sides of the tins. Gently press the sides to fit, trim the edges, then wrap the tins in plastic wrap and refrigerate for 30 minutes.

3 **Line each of the pastry shells** with a crumpled piece of baking paper and fill with baking beads or uncooked rice. Blind bake the pastry for 10 minutes, then remove the paper and beads and bake for a further 5 minutes, or until the pastry is golden. Allow to cool.

4 **To make the grapefruit curd,** combine the butter, eggs, grapefruit juice, zest and sugar in a heatproof bowl. Place over a saucepan of simmering water and stir constantly for 10–15 minutes, or until the mixture thickens. Set aside to cool. Spoon the curd into the tart shells, smoothing the top. Place in the refrigerator for 30 minutes, or until completely cold.

5 **To make the meringue,** whisk the egg whites in a clean, dry bowl until soft peaks form. Add the sugar, 1 tablespoon at a time, whisking well after each addition. Whisk until the mixture is stiff and glossy and the sugar has dissolved. Add the cornflour, whisking to mix well.

6 **Place the mixture** in a piping bag fitted with a 2 cm (¾ inch) plain nozzle. Remove tartlets from the fridge and pipe meringue over the curd. Bake 10 minutes, or until meringue is golden. Dust with icing sugar. Garnish with grated lemon zest.

MINI PASSIONFRUIT ALMOND CAKES WITH LIME GLAZE

MAKES 8

60 g (2¼ oz/⅓ cup) ground almonds

2 tablespoons plain (all-purpose) flour, sifted

100 g (3½ oz) icing (confectioners') sugar, plus extra to dust

1 teaspoon finely grated lime zest

pulp from 1 passionfruit

120 g (4¼ oz) unsalted butter, melted

2 eggs, at room temperature

2 tablespoons lime juice

1 **Preheat the oven** to 170°C (325°F/Gas 3). Lightly grease eight 30 ml (1 oz) patty tins.

2 **Place the ground almonds,** flour, 60 g (2¼ oz) icing sugar, lime zest, passionfruit pulp and half the butter in a bowl.

3 **Separate the eggs,** reserve 1 egg yolk and discard the other. Beat the egg whites in a clean, dry bowl using electric beaters to soft peaks. Gently fold into the almond mixture. Spoon into prepared patty tins and bake for 12–15 minutes, or until the cakes are puffed and golden.

4 **Meanwhile,** place the lime juice, remaining butter and sifted remaining icing sugar in a small saucepan, and heat to a simmer, stirring until all the sugar has dissolved.

5 **Remove from the heat** and cool slightly, then whisk in the reserved egg yolk. Return to very low heat and stir for 5 minutes, or until thickened. Do not boil. Leave in the tin for 5 minutes, then gently remove.

6 **Serve two cakes per person,** dusted with extra icing sugar and drizzled with a little lime curd. Serve with cream or ice cream, if desired.

LITTLE LEMON TARTS

MAKES 24

250 g (9 oz/2 cups) plain (all-purpose) flour

pinch of salt

125 g (4½ oz) unsalted butter, chopped

2 teaspoons caster (superfine) sugar

1 teaspoon lemon zest

1 egg yolk

2–3 tablespoons ice water

candied lemon strips, to decorate

FILLING

125 g (1½ oz/½ cup) cream cheese, softened

115 g (4 oz/½ cup) caster (superfine) sugar

2 egg yolks

2 tablespoons lemon juice

½ tablespoon sweetened condensed milk

1 **Preheat the oven** to 180°C (350°F/Gas 4). Grease two 12-cup cupcake tins. Sift flour and salt into bowl. Rub butter into the flour mixture. Add the sugar, lemon zest, egg yolk and water and mix with a knife. Gently knead onto a lightly floured surface until smooth. Cover in plastic wrap and refrigerate for 10 minutes.

2 **To make filling,** using electric beaters, beat cream cheese, sugar and egg yolks until smooth and thickened. Add lemon juice and condensed milk and beat until well combined.

3 **Roll out the dough** between sheets of baking paper to 3 mm (⅛ inch) thickness. Using a 7 cm (2¾ inch) fluted, round cutter, cut rounds from pastry. Gently press pastry into paper cases. Lightly prick each round 3 times with a fork and bake for 10 minutes or until just starting to turn golden.

4 **Remove from the oven** and spoon 2 teaspoons of filling into each case. Return to the oven for another 5 minutes or until filling has set. Allow tarts to cool slightly before removing from tins. Garnish with candied lemon strips, if desired.

RASPBERRY AND PASSIONFRUIT CAKES

MAKES 6

30 g (1 oz/¼ cup) plain (all-purpose) flour

90 g (3¼ oz/¾ cup) self-raising flour

140 g (4⅔ oz/¾ cup) ground almonds

185 g (6½ oz) unsalted butter

250 g (9 oz/1 cup) caster (superfine) sugar

125 g (4½ oz/½ cup) fresh passionfruit pulp

2 teaspoons natural vanilla extract

2 eggs

125 g (4½ oz/1 cup) frozen or fresh raspberries

icing (confectioners') sugar, to dust

1 **Preheat the oven** to 180°C (350°F/Gas 4). Grease six 160 ml (5¼ fl oz) mini heart-shaped tins.

2 **Combine the plain flour,** self-raising flour and ground almonds in a large bowl. Make a well in the centre.

3 **Put the butter,** sugar, pulp and vanilla extract in a saucepan. Stir over low heat until the butter has melted and the mixture is smooth.

4 **Whisk the butter mixture** into the dry ingredients. Whisk in the eggs until smooth.

5 **Pour the mixture** into the tins. Drop the raspberries on top, pushing them just below the surface.

6 **Bake for 25 minutes,** or until lightly golden. Set aside for 10 minutes, then turn out onto a wire rack to cool. Dust with icing sugar to serve.

FLOURLESS CHOCOLATE CAKES

MAKES 8

250 g (9 oz/1²/₃ cups) dark chocolate, chopped

100 g (3½ oz/scant ½ cup) caster (superfine) sugar

100 g (3½ oz) unsalted butter, cubed

125 g (4½ oz/1 heaped cup) ground hazelnuts

5 eggs, separated

icing (confectioners') sugar, to dust

1 **Preheat the oven** to 180°C (350°F/Gas 4). Grease eight 125 ml (4 fl oz/½ cup) mini flower-shaped tins and line the bases with baking paper.

2 **Place the chocolate,** sugar and butter in a heatproof bowl. Sit the bowl over a saucepan of simmering water, making sure the base of the bowl doesn't touch the water. Stir occasionally. Remove from the heat and stir well.

3 **Transfer the chocolate mixture** to a large bowl. Stir in the hazelnuts, then beat in the egg yolks, one at a time, mixing well after each addition.

4 **In a clean, dry bowl,** whisk the egg whites until stiff peaks form. Gently fold into the chocolate using a metal spoon or spatula. Pour the mixture into the tins.

5 **Bake** for 30-40 minutes, or until a skewer inserted into the centre of a cake comes out clean. Leave to cool completely in the tin, then turn out and dust with icing sugar.

BAKLAVA

MAKES 18

560 g (1 lb 4 oz/2¼ cups) caster (superfine) sugar
1½ teaspoons lemon zest
90 g (3¼ oz/¼ cup) honey
3 tablespoons lemon juice
2 tablespoons orange blossom water
200 g (7 oz/2 cups) walnuts, finely chopped
200 g (7 oz/1⅓ cups) pistachio nuts, finely chopped
200 g (7 oz/1⅓ cups) almonds, finely chopped
2 tablespoons caster (superfine) sugar, extra
2 teaspoons ground cinnamon
375 g (13 oz) filo pastry
200 g (7 oz) unsalted butter, melted

1 **Put sugar,** lemon zest and 375 ml (13 fl oz/1½ cups) water in a pan. Stir over high heat until sugar dissolves, then boil for 5 minutes. Reduce the heat. Simmer for 5 minutes. Add the honey, lemon juice and orange blossom water and cook for 2 minutes. Remove from heat. Refrigerate.

2 **Preheat the oven** to 170°C (325°F/Gas 3).

3 **Combine the nuts,** extra sugar and cinnamon.

4 **Lightly grease** a 27 x 30 cm (10½ x 12 inch) baking dish. Cover the base with a single layer of filo pastry and brush lightly with melted butter, folding in any overhanging edges. Continue to layer 10 more sheets of filo. Store the remaining filo under a damp tea towel (dish towel). Sprinkle half the nuts over the pastry and pat down. Repeat the layering and buttering of five more filo sheets, sprinkle with the rest of the nuts, then layer and butter the remaining filo, brushing the top with butter and pat down. Score into large diamonds. Pour any remaining butter over the top.

5 **Bake for 30 minutes,** then reduce the heat to 150°C (300°F/Gas 2) and cook for 30 minutes. Immediately cut through the original diamond markings, then strain the syrup over the top. Refrigerate before serving.

NEENISH TARTS

MAKES 12

BUTTERCREAM ICING (FROSTING)

60 g (2¼ oz) unsalted butter

60 g (2¼ oz/½ cup) icing
(confectioners') sugar, sifted

15 ml (½ fl oz/1 tablespoon) milk

few drops imitation rum essence
(optional)

12 precooked tartlet cases

1 tablespoon raspberry jam

125 g (4½ oz/1 cup) icing
(confectioners') sugar, extra

1 teaspoon natural vanilla extract

3 teaspoons hot water

few drops pink food colouring

1 **To make buttercream icing (frosting)**, place butter into small mixing bowl. Using electric beaters, beat on high speed for 1 minute. Add ½ cup sugar, milk and essence, beat until light and creamy.

2 **Place ½ teaspoon jam** into each tartlet and spread over base. Top jam with 2 teaspoons buttercream mixture, creating a smooth surface with the back of a teaspoon.

3 **Sift the remaining icing sugar** into small mixing bowl, make a well in centre. Add the essence and water. Using a flat-bladed knife, stir until the mixture is smooth. Divide the mixture into two portions. Leave one portion plain and tint the remaining portion pink.

4 **Spread 1 teaspoon** of plain icing over half of each tartlet and allow to set. Spread 1 teaspoon of pink icing over the remaining half of each tartlet and allow to set.

RUM BABA WITH APRICOT JAM

MAKES 10

185 g (6½ oz/1½ cups) plain (all-purpose) flour

2 teaspoons dried yeast

¼ teaspoon salt

2 teaspoons sugar

80 ml (2¾ fl oz/⅓ cup) lukewarm milk

80 g (2¾ oz) unsalted butter

3 eggs, lightly beaten

500 ml (16 fl oz/2 cups) water

375 g (13 oz/1½ cups) caster (superfine) sugar

80 ml (2¾ fl oz/⅓ cup) dark rum

240 g (8½ oz/¾ cup) apricot jam

2 tablespoons dark rum, extra

1 Lightly brush ten 125 ml (4 fl oz/½-cup) dariole moulds with oil. Place 1 tablespoon of the flour and the yeast, salt, sugar and milk in a small bowl. Cover with plastic wrap and leave in a warm place for 10 minutes, or until the mixture is foamy. Using your fingertips, rub butter into the remaining flour in a large mixing bowl, until it resembles fine breadcrumbs.

2 Add the yeast mixture and eggs to the flour mixture. Beat with a spoon for 2 minutes, until smooth and glossy. Scrape the mixture down the side of the bowl. Cover and leave in a warm place for 1½ hours, until well risen.

3 Preheat the oven to 210°C (415°F/Gas 6–7). Using a wooden spoon, beat the mixture again for 2 minutes. Divide the mixture evenly between prepared tins. Set aside, covered with plastic wrap, for another 30 minutes, until the dough is well risen.

4 Bake for 20 minutes, or until golden brown. Meanwhile, combine the water and sugar in a medium saucepan. Stir over medium heat without boiling until the sugar has dissolved. Bring to the boil then reduce heat slightly and simmer, without stirring, for 15 minutes. Remove from heat, cool slightly and add the rum.

5 Turn out onto a wire rack placed over a shallow oven tray. Brush the warm babas generously with warm rum syrup until they are well soaked. Strain excess syrup to remove any crumbs if necessary and reserve syrup.

6 Heat the jam in a small saucepan or in the microwave and strain through a fine sieve. Add the extra rum, stir to combine and brush the warm jam all over the babas to glaze. Place one or two babas on each plate, drizzle a pool of reserved syrup around them and serve.

RICE FLOUR AND MADEIRA FRIANDS

MAKES 18

250 g (9 oz) unsalted butter, softened

350 g (12 oz/1½ cups) caster (superfine) sugar

8 eggs

1 teaspoon finely grated orange zest

80 g (2¾ oz/¾ cup) ground almonds

300 g (10½ oz/1¾ cups) rice flour, sifted

60 ml (2 fl oz/¼ cup) madeira or sherry

80 g (2¾ oz/½ cup) chopped blanched almonds

icing (confectioners') sugar, for dusting

whipped cream and berries, to serve

1 Preheat the oven to 170°C (325°F/Gas 3). Grease eighteen 125 ml (4 fl oz/½ cup) friand tins.

2 Cream butter and sugar in a bowl using electric beaters until pale and fluffy. Add the eggs one at a time, beating well after each addition, then add the orange zest and continue to beat for 5 minutes. Combine ground almonds and rice flour and fold into the butter mixture, in three stages, alternately with the madeira, until just combined.

3 Spoon the mixture into the prepared tins and sprinkle the almonds over each cupcake. Bake for 25–30 minutes, or until golden and a skewer inserted into the centre of a friand comes out clean. Leave in the tins for 5 minutes, then turn out onto a wire rack to cool. Dust with icing sugar and serve with whipped cream and berries.

Note: The friands will keep, stored in an airtight container, for up to 4 days, or frozen for up to 3 months.

HONEY AND COCONUT CAKES

MAKES 6

125 g (4½ oz) unsalted butter, softened

140 g (4½ oz/⅔ cup) raw (demerara) sugar

2 large eggs, lightly beaten

1 teaspoon natural vanilla extract

90 g (3¼ oz/¼ cup) honey

45 g (1½ oz/½ cup) desiccated coconut

220 g (7 oz/1¾ cups) self-raising flour

1 teaspoon ground nutmeg

¼ teaspoon ground cinnamon

¼ teaspoon ground allspice

125 ml (4 fl oz/½ cup) milk

HONEY AND CREAM CHEESE ICING (FROSTING)

125 g (4½ oz) cream cheese, softened

60 g (2¼ oz/½ cup) icing (confectioners') sugar

1 tablespoon honey

1 **Preheat the oven** to 180°C (350°F/Gas 4). Lightly grease six 10 cm (4 inch) round cake tins and line the bases with baking paper.

2 **Beat the butter** and sugar in a bowl using electric beaters until creamy. Add the eggs gradually, beating well after each addition. Add the vanilla extract and honey. Beat until well combined.

3 **Add the desiccated coconut.** Using a metal spoon, fold in the sifted flour and spices and add the milk. Stir until just combined and the mixture is almost smooth. Spoon into the prepared tins and smooth the surface.

4 **Bake for 30 to 35 minutes,** or until lightly golden. Leave the cake in the tin for 10 minutes before turning out onto a wire rack to cool completely. Remove the baking paper from the cake.

5 **To make the icing,** beat the softened cream cheese in a bowl using electric beaters until creamy. Add the sifted icing sugar and honey, beating for 3 minutes or until the mixture is smooth and fluffy. Spread the icing over the whole cake using a flat-bladed knife.

Note: These cakes can be stored for 4 days in an airtight container.

LAMINGTONS

MAKES 16

185 g (6½ oz/1½ cups) self-raising flour

40 g (1½ oz/⅓ cup) cornflour
(cornstarch)

185 g (6½ oz) unsalted butter, softened

230 g (8½ oz/1 cup) caster (superfine)
sugar

2 teaspoons natural vanilla extract

3 eggs, lightly beaten

125 ml (4 fl oz/½ cup) milk

ICING (FROSTING)

500 g (1 lb 2 oz/4 cups) icing
(confectioners') sugar

40 g (1½ oz/⅓ cup) unsweetened
cocoa powder

30 g (1 oz) unsalted butter, melted

170 ml (5½ fl oz/⅔ cup) milk

270 g (9½ oz/3 cups) desiccated
coconut

1   **Preheat the oven** to 180°C (350°F/Gas 4). Grease a shallow 23 cm (9 inch) square cake tin and line the base and sides with baking paper.

2   **Sift the flour** and cornflour into a bowl. Add the butter, sugar, vanilla, egg and milk. Using electric beaters, beat for 3 minutes. Pour into the tin.

3   **Bake for 50–55 minutes,** or until lightly golden. Leave for 3 minutes, then turn out onto a wire rack to cool.

4   **Using a knife,** trim the crusts from the sides. Cut the cake into 16 squares.

5   **To make the icing (frosting),** sift the icing sugar and cocoa into a heatproof bowl and add the butter and milk. Stand over a saucepan of simmering water and stir until the icing is smooth, then remove from the heat.

6   **Place 90 g** (3¼ oz/1 cup) of the coconut in a bowl. Using two forks, roll a piece of cake in chocolate icing, then hold over the bowl to allow the excess to drain.

7   **Roll the cake in coconut,** then place on a wire rack. Repeat with the remaining cake.

FINGER BUNS

MAKES 12

500 g (1 lb 2 oz/4 cups) plain (all-purpose) flour

35 g (1¼ oz/⅓ cup) milk powder

1 tablespoon dried yeast

115 g (4 oz/½ cup) caster (superfine) sugar

60 g (2¼ oz/½ cup) sultanas (golden raisins)

60 g (2¼ oz) unsalted butter, melted

1 egg, lightly beaten

1 egg yolk, extra, to glaze

GLACÉ ICING (FROSTING)

155 g (5½ oz/1¼ cups) icing (confectioners') sugar

20 g (¾ oz) unsalted butter, melted

pink food colouring

1 Mix 375 g (13 oz/3 cups) of the flour with the milk powder, yeast, sugar, sultanas and ½ teaspoon salt in a large bowl. Make a well in the centre. Combine the butter, egg and 250 ml (9 fl oz/1 cup) warm water and add all at once to the flour. Stir for 2 minutes, or until well combined. Add enough of the remaining flour to make a soft dough.

2 Turn out onto a lightly floured surface. Knead for 10 minutes, or until the dough is smooth and elastic, adding more flour if necessary. Place in a large lightly oiled bowl and brush with oil. Cover with plastic wrap and leave in a warm place for 1 hour, or until well risen.

3 Lightly grease two large baking trays. Preheat oven to 180°C (350°F/Gas 4). Punch down the dough and knead for 1 minute. Divide into 12 pieces. Shape each into a 15 cm (6 inch) long oval. Put on the trays 5 cm (2 inches) apart. Cover with plastic wrap and set aside in a warm place for 20–25 minutes, or until well risen.

4 Mix the extra egg yolk with 1½ teaspoons water and brush over the dough. Bake for 12–15 minutes, or until firm and golden. Transfer to a wire rack to cool.

5 To make the icing (frosting), stir the icing sugar, 2–3 teaspoons water and the melted butter together in a bowl until smooth. Mix in the food colouring and spread over the tops of the buns. Finger buns are delicious buttered.

SUNKEN CHOCOLATE DESSERT CAKES

SERVES 4

1 tablespoon melted unsalted butter

115 g (4 oz/½ cup) caster (superfine) sugar, plus 1 tablespoon extra

150 g (5½ oz/1 cup) dark chocolate, chopped

125 g (4½ oz) butter

3 eggs

30 g (1 oz/¼ cup) plain (all-purpose) flour

ice cream, to serve

1 Preheat the oven to 180°C (350°F/Gas 4). Grease four 250 ml (9 fl oz/1 cup) ramekins with the melted butter and coat lightly with the extra sugar.

2 Put the chocolate and butter in a small heatproof bowl. Sit the bowl over a small saucepan of simmering water, stirring frequently until the chocolate and butter have melted. Take care that the base of the bowl doesn't touch the water. Remove from the heat.

3 Whisk the eggs and sugar in a bowl using electric beaters until pale and thick. Sift the flour onto the egg mixture. Whisk the flour into the mixture. Whisk in the melted chocolate.

4 Divide the batter between the prepared ramekins and place on a baking tray. Bake for 30 to 35 minutes, or until set and firm to touch. Allow to cool in the ramekins for 10 minutes before turning out onto serving plates (if they are reluctant to come out, run a knife around the inside edge of the ramekins to loosen them). Alternatively, serve them in the ramekins, dusted with icing sugar. Serve warm with ice cream.

CARDAMOM, ORANGE AND PLUM DESSERT CAKES

MAKES 8

185 g (6½ oz) unsalted butter, chopped

95 g (3¼ oz/½ cup) soft brown sugar

115 g (4 oz/½ cup) caster (superfine) sugar

3 eggs

1 teaspoon finely grated orange zest

310 g (11 oz/2½ cups) self-raising flour, sifted

1 teaspoon ground cardamom

185 ml (6 fl oz/¾ cup) milk

4 tinned plums, drained and patted dry, cut in half

1 tablespoon raw (demerara) sugar

thick (double/heavy) cream, to serve

1 **Preheat the oven** to 180°C (350°F/Gas 4). Lightly grease eight 250 ml (9 fl oz/1 cup) ceramic ramekins and dust with flour, shaking out any excess flour.

2 **Cream the butter** and sugars in a bowl using electric beaters until pale and fluffy. Add the eggs, one at a time and beating well after each addition, then stir in the orange zest. Fold the flour and cardamom into the butter mixture alternately with the milk until combined and smooth.

3 **Divide the mixture** between the ramekins and place a plum half, cut side down, on top of the batter. Sprinkle with raw sugar, place the ramekins on a baking tray and bake for 30 to 35 minutes, or until golden and firm to the touch. Serve warm or at room temperature with thick cream.

CUPCAKES

COFFEE CUPCAKES

MAKES 24

195 g (6¾ oz) unsalted butter, softened

125 g (4½ oz/⅔ cup) soft brown sugar

2 eggs

1 tablespoon coffee and
   chicory essence

155 g (5½ oz/1¼ cups) self-raising flour

100 ml (3½ fl oz) buttermilk

125 g (4½ oz/1 cup) icing
   (confectioners') sugar

chocolate-coated coffee beans,
   to decorate

cocoa powder, for dusting

1   **Preheat the oven** to 150°C (300°F/Gas 2). Line two 12-hole standard cupcake trays with paper cases. Beat 185g (6½ oz) of the butter and the brown sugar with electric beaters until light and creamy. Add eggs one at a time, beating well after each addition. Mix in 3 teaspoons of the coffee and chicory essence.

2   **Fold the flour** and a pinch of salt alternately with the buttermilk into the creamed mixture until combined. Spoon evenly into the paper cake cases and bake for 25–30 minutes, or until just springy to the touch. Leave to cool in the tins.

3   **To make the icing (frosting),** combine the remaining butter, remaining essence, the icing sugar and 1½ tablespoons boiling water in a small mixing bowl. Spread a little icing over each cupcake with a flat-bladed knife until evenly covered. Dust with sifted cocoa powder.

INDIVIDUAL WHITE CHOCOLATE CUPCAKES

MAKES 12

125 g (4½ oz) unsalted butter, softened

185 g (6½ oz/¾ cup) caster (superfine) sugar

2 eggs, lightly beaten

1 teaspoon natural vanilla extract

250 g (9 oz/2 cups) self-raising flour, sifted

125 ml (4 fl oz/½ cup) buttermilk

280 g (10 oz/1¼ cups) white chocolate chips

1 Preheat the oven to 170°C (325°F/Gas 3). Lightly grease a 12-hole standard cupcake tray.

2 Place the butter and sugar in a large mixing bowl. Using electric beaters, beat until pale and creamy. Gradually add the beaten eggs, beating well after each addition. Add the vanilla extract and beat until well combined. Fold in the flour alternately with the buttermilk, then fold in the chocolate chips.

3 Fill each muffin hole three-quarters full with the mixture and bake for 20 minutes, or until a skewer comes out clean when inserted in the centre of each cake. Leave in the tin for 5 minutes before turning out onto a wire rack to cool completely. Use a flat-bladed knife to loosen around the edges of the cakes if they stick.

JAFFA CUPCAKES

MAKES 12

185 g (6½ oz) unsalted butter

115 g (4 oz/½ cup) caster (superfine) sugar

2 eggs

1 teaspoon grated orange zest

125 g (4½ oz/½ cup) sour cream

215 g (7½ oz/1¾cups) self-raising flour, sifted

40 g (1½ oz/⅓ cup) cocoa powder, sifted

80 ml (2½ fl oz/⅓ cup) orange juice

extra orange zest, for decoration

ICING (FROSTING)

100 g (3½ oz/⅔ cup) dark chocolate, chopped

50 g (1¾ oz) unsalted butter

30 g (1 oz/¼ cup) icing (confectioners') sugar

1 **Preheat the oven** to 180°C (350°F/Gas 4). Lightly grease a 12-hole standard muffin tin.

2 **Beat butter** and sugar with electric beaters until light and creamy. Add eggs gradually, beating thoroughly after each addition. Add the zest and sour cream and beat to combine.

3 **Add the sifted ingredients** alternately with orange juice and beat mixture until smooth.

4 **Pour the mixture** into the prepared tin and smooth the surface. Alternately, place in paper cases. Bake for 25 minutes or until a skewer comes out clean when inserted in to the centre of a cake.

5 **Leave the cupcakes** in the tin for 10 minutes before turning onto a wire rack to cool.

6 **To make icing (frosting),** place chocolate in a bowl over barely simmering water, making sure the base doesn't touch the water. Stir until chocolate has melted, then remove from the heat. Beat butter and sugar with electric beaters until light and creamy. Add the chocolate and stir until combined. Spread evenly over each cupcake and top with extra orange zest.

LITTLE JAM-FILLED CUPCAKES

MAKES 12

280 g (10 oz/2¼ cups) self-raising flour

170 g (6 oz/¾ cup) caster (superfine) sugar

250 ml (9 fl oz/1 cup) milk

2 eggs, lightly beaten

½ teaspoon natural vanilla extract

75 g (2½ oz) unsalted butter, melted

80 g (2¾ oz/¼ cup) strawberry jam

12 small strawberries, hulled (optional)

icing (confectioners') sugar, for dusting

1   Preheat the oven to 200°C (400°F/Gas 6). Lightly grease a 12-hole standard muffin tin.

2   Sift the flour into a bowl, add the sugar and stir to combine. Make a well in the centre. Put the milk, eggs, vanilla and butter in a bowl, whisking to combine. Pour into the well and, using a metal spoon, gradually fold the milk mixture into the flour mixture until just combined.

3   Divide three-quarters of the cake batter between the muffin holes. Top each with 1 teaspoon of the jam and cover with the remaining cake batter. Gently press a strawberry into the centre, if desired.

4   Bake for 20 minutes, or until light golden. Cool in the tin for 5 minutes, then turn out onto a wire rack to cool completely. Dust with icing sugar to serve.

RAISIN BRAN CUPCAKES

MAKES 20

110 g (3¾oz/1½ cups) unprocessed bran

150 g (5½ oz/1 cup) wholemeal flour

60 g (2¼ oz/½ cup) raisins

30 g (1 oz/¼ cup) chopped walnuts

1 teaspoon bicarbonate of soda
   (baking soda)

1 teaspoon ground cinnamon

1 teaspoon ground nutmeg

1 egg, beaten

180 g (6 oz/½ cup) honey

2 tablespoons oil

1 teaspoon natural vanilla extract

185 ml (6 fl oz/¾ cup) low-fat milk

1 **Preheat the oven** to 200°C (400°F/Gas 6). Line two 10-hole cupcake tins with paper cases.

2 **Mix the bran,** flour, raisins, nuts, bicarbonate and spices. Combine the egg, honey, oil, vanilla and milk and stir thoroughly. Pour slowly into mixed dry ingredients. Stir but don't overmix.

3 **Spoon mixture** evenly into paper cases. Bake for about 15 minutes until puffed and firm, or until a skewer inserted in the centre of a cake comes out clean. Leave in the tin for 5 minutes, then turn out onto a wire rack to cool completely. Remove paper cases to serve.

BLUEBERRY SEMOLINA CUPCAKES

MAKES 12

30 g (1 oz/¼ cup) self-raising flour

40 g (1½ oz/⅓ cup) semolina

230 g (8 oz/1 cup) caster (superfine) sugar

25 g (1 oz/¼ cup) ground almonds

½ teaspoon finely grated lemon zest

4 egg whites, lightly beaten

125 g (4½ oz) unsalted butter, melted

80 g (2¾ oz/½ cup) blueberries

45 g (1½ oz/½ cup) flaked almonds

icing (confectioners') sugar, for dusting

1 **Preheat the oven** to 170°C (325°F/Gas 3). Line a 12-hole standard cupcake tray with paper cases.

2 **Sift the flour** and semolina into a large bowl and add the sugar, ground almonds and lemon zest and stir to combine. Add the egg whites and, using electric beaters, beat until the ingredients are combined. Pour in the melted butter and continue to beat until smooth and well combined. Add the blueberries and fold in to just combine, then spoon the batter into the paper cases.

3 **Sprinkle the flaked** almonds over the cakes and bake for 30 minutes, or until a skewer inserted in the centre of a cake comes out clean. Turn out onto a wire rack to cool. Dust with icing sugar to serve.

Note: The blueberry cakes are best served on the day they are made.

GINGER CUPCAKES WITH CHOCOLATE CENTRES

MAKES 12

100 g (3½ oz) unsalted butter, softened

125 g (4½ oz/⅔ cup) soft brown sugar

115 g (4 oz/⅓ cup) treacle or dark corn syrup

2 eggs

125 g (4½ oz/1 cup) self-raising flour

85 g (3 oz/⅔ cup) plain (all-purpose) flour

2 teaspoons ground cinnamon

1 tablespoon ground ginger

60 ml (2 fl oz/¼ cup) buttermilk

GINGER GANACHE

100 g (3½ oz/⅔ cup) good-quality dark chocolate, chopped

60 ml (2 fl oz/¼ cup) pouring cream

1 tablespoon finely chopped glacé ginger

1 **Preheat the oven** to 180°C (350°F/Gas 4). Line a 12-hole standard cupcake tray with paper cases.

2 **To make the ginger ganache,** put the chocolate in a small heatproof bowl. Heat the cream until almost boiling, then pour over the chocolate and stir until it has melted and the mixture is smooth. Stir in the ginger. Cool to room temperature, then chill in the refrigerator until firm. Divide the mixture into 12 equal portions and roll each into a ball. Freeze until required.

3 **Cream the butter,** sugar and treacle in a small bowl using electric beaters until pale and fluffy. Add the eggs one at a time, beating well after each addition. Transfer to a large bowl. Sift the flours and spices into a bowl, then fold into the butter mixture alternately with the buttermilk.

4 **Divide three-quarters** of the mixture between the paper cases. Top each with a ball of frozen ginger ganache, then spread the remaining mixture over the top of the ganache to cover. Bake for 25–30 minutes, or until deep golden (the cakes cannot be tested with a skewer as the centres will be molten). Leave to cool for 5 minutes, then turn out onto a wire rack to cool completely. Remove the paper cases and serve warm.

Note: These ginger cakes will keep, stored in an airtight container, for up to 4 days, or up to 3 months in the freezer.

SOUR CREAM CUPCAKES

MAKES 22

150 g (5½ oz) unsalted butter

125 g (4½ oz/½ cup) caster (superfine) sugar

1 teaspoon natural vanilla extract

2 eggs, lightly beaten

160 g (5½ oz/^{2}/$_3$ cup) sour cream

155 g (5½ oz/1¼ cups) self-raising flour

45 g (1½ oz/¼ cup) rice flour

ready-made lemon butter, for topping

1 Preheat the oven to 180°C (350°F/Gas 4). Line two deep, 12-hole cupcake tins with paper cases.

2 Beat the butter and sugar in a large bowl until light and creamy. Gradually beat in the vanilla and eggs.

3 Use a large metal spoon to fold in the sour cream and combined sifted flours, until just smooth.

4 Spoon the mixture into the paper cases. Bake for 15–20 minutes, or until the cupcakes are golden on top. Test a few with a skewer — if it comes out clean they are cooked. Leave in the tin for 5 minutes, then turn out onto a wire rack to cool. Top with a little lemon butter.

SULTANA CUPCAKES

MAKES 16–18

155 g (5½ oz) unsalted butter

145 g (5 oz/⅔ cup) caster (superfine) sugar

1 teaspoon natural vanilla extract

2 eggs

185 g (6½ oz/1½ cups) self-raising flour

pinch salt

90 g (3¼ oz/¾ cup) sultanas (golden raisins)

1 **Preheat the oven** to 200°C (400°F/Gas 6). Line two 9-hole cupcake tins with paper cases.

2 **Beat the butter** with the sugar and vanilla until light and fluffy.

3 **Add the eggs** one at a time. Mix together the remaining ingredients and add to the mixture, blend until smooth.

4 **Divide the mixture** evenly into paper cases, filling them about half way up. Bake for 15 minutes, or until a skewer inserted in the centre of a cake comes out clean. Leave in the tin for 5 minutes then turn out onto a rack to cool completely.

INDIVIDUAL MILK CHOCOLATE CUPCAKES

MAKES 12

75 g (2¾ oz) unsalted butter

75 g (2¾ oz/½ cup) milk chocolate, chopped

80 g (2¾ oz/⅓ cup) firmly packed brown sugar

2 eggs, lightly beaten

60 g (2¼ oz/½ cup) self-raising flour, sifted

GANACHE

80 g (2¾ oz/heaped ½ cup) milk chocolate, chopped

2 tablespoons thick (double/heavy) cream

1   Preheat the oven to 160°C (315°F/ Gas 2–3). Line a flat-bottomed 12-hole cupcake tray with paper cases. Put the butter and chocolate in a heatproof bowl and place over a saucepan of simmering water—make sure the base of the bowl doesn't touch the water. Stir until melted and combined. Remove the bowl from the heat, add the sugar and egg and mix. Stir in the flour.

2   Transfer the mixture to a measuring bowl and pour into the paper cases. Bake for 20–25 minutes, or until a skewer inserted in the centre of a cake comes out clean. Leave in the tin for 10 minutes, then transfer to a wire rack to cool.

3   To make the ganache, place the chocolate and cream in a heatproof bowl. Place over a saucepan of simmering water, making sure that the base of the bowl doesn't touch the water. Once the chocolate has almost melted, remove the bowl from the heat and stir until the remaining chocolate has melted and the mixture is smooth. Allow to cool for about 8 minutes, or until thickened slightly. Return cakes to the cold cupcake tin to keep them stable while you spread one heaped teaspoon of ganache over the top.

SOUR CHERRY CUPCAKES

MAKES 8

125 g (4½ oz) unsalted butter, softened

185 g (6½ oz/¾ cup) caster (superfine) sugar

2 eggs, lightly beaten

55 g (3¼ oz/½ cup) ground almonds

125 g (4½ oz/1 cup) self-raising flour

60 g (2¼ oz/½ cup) plain (all-purpose) flour

125 ml (4 fl oz/½ cup) milk

680 g (1 lb 8 oz) jar pitted morello cherries, well drained

icing (confectioners') sugar, to dust

1 **Preheat the oven** to 180°C (350°F/Gas 4). Brush one 8-cup cupcake tin with melted butter or oil. Beat the butter and sugar with electric beaters until pale. Add the beaten egg gradually, beating well after each addition.

2 **Stir in the ground almonds,** then fold in the sifted flours alternately with the milk. Gently fold in the cherries.

3 **Spoon the mixture** into the prepared tin and smooth the surface. Bake for 35 minutes, or until a skewer comes out clean when inserted in the centre of a cake. Leave to cool in the tin for 10 minutes before turning out onto a wire rack to cool. Dust with icing sugar before serving.

SAFFRON SPICE CUPCAKES

MAKES 8

250 ml (9 fl oz/1 cup) freshly squeezed orange juice

1 tablespoon finely grated orange zest

¼ teaspoon saffron threads

3 eggs

155 g (5½ oz/1¼ cups) icing (confectioners') sugar

250 g (9 oz/2 cups) self-raising flour

370 g (12¾ oz/3⅔ cups) ground almonds

125 g (4½ oz) unsalted butter, melted

icing (confectioners') sugar, extra, to dust

thick (double/heavy) cream, to serve

1 **Preheat the oven** to 180°C (350°F/Gas 4). Prepare an 8-hole cupcake tin and line with paper cases. Combine the orange juice, zest and saffron in a small saucepan and bring to the boil. Lower the heat and simmer for 1 minute. Leave to cool.

2 **Beat the eggs** and icing sugar with electric beaters until light and creamy. Fold in sifted flour, almonds, orange juice mixture and butter with a metal spoon until just combined and the mixture is just smooth. Spoon the mixture into the prepared tin.

3 **Bake for 40 minutes,** or until a skewer comes out clean when inserted in the centre of a cake. Leave in the tin for 10 minutes before turning onto a wire rack to cool. Dust with a little icing sugar and serve with cream.

PUMPKIN CUPCAKES

MAKES 12

185 g (6½ oz/1½ cups) self-raising flour

½ teaspoon salt

¼ teaspoon ground nutmeg

¼ teaspoon mixed (pumpkin pie) spice

115 g (4 oz/½ cup) firmly packed brown sugar

60 g (2¼ oz/½ cup) sultanas (golden raisins)

1 egg

60 ml (2 fl oz/¼ cup) vegetable oil

125 g (4½ oz/½ cup) mashed, drained, cooked pumpkin

125 ml (4 fl oz/½ cup) milk

1   **Preheat the oven** to 200°C (400°F/Gas 6). Prepare a 12-hole cupcake tin and line with paper cases.

2   **Sift the flour**, salt and spices into a bowl. Stir in the sugar and sultanas.

3   **Beat the egg**, add the oil, pumpkin and milk and mix thoroughly. Add this mixture to the dry ingredients and stir thoroughly.

4   **Divide the mixture** evenly into the paper cases and bake for 20–25 minutes or until a skewer inserted in the centre of a cake comes out clean. Leave in the tin for 5 minutes then turn out onto a wire rack to cool completely.

5   **These cupcakes** are best served on the day that they are made.

LEMON CUPCAKES

MAKES 6

180 g (6 oz) unsalted butter, softened

185 g (6½ oz/¾ cup) caster (superfine) sugar

3 eggs, beaten

165 g (5½ oz/1⅓ cups) self-raising flour, sifted

2 teaspoons finely grated lemon zest

1 teaspoon lemon juice

2 teaspoons caster (superfine) sugar, extra, to sprinkle

icing (confectioners') sugar, to dust

1 tablespoon lemon zest

1 **Preheat the oven** to 160°C (315°F/ Gas 2–3). Prepare a 6-hole cupcake tin and line with paper cases.

2 **Beat the butter** and sugar with electric beaters until pale and creamy. Add the eggs gradually, beating well after each addition. Fold in the flour, lemon zest and juice until combined.

3 **When smooth,** divide evenly into the prepared tin and level the surface.

4 **Sprinkle the extra sugar** over the top. Bake for about 35 minutes, or until a skewer comes out clean when inserted in the centre of a cake. Allow to cool for 10 minutes in the tin before turning out onto a wire rack to cool completely. Dust with icing sugar and garnish with lemon zest.

FAIRY CUPCAKES

MAKES 36

150 g (5 oz) unsalted butter

¾ cup caster sugar

2 eggs, lightly beaten

1 teaspoon vanilla essence

2 teaspoons lemon juice

250 g (9 oz/2 cups) self-raising flour

125 ml (4 fl oz/½ cup) milk

80 g (2oz/½ cup) raspberry jam

310 ml (11 fl oz/1¼ cups) cream, whipped

icing sugar, for decoration

1 Preheat the oven to 180°C (350°F/Gas 4). Prepare a 12-hole cupcake tin and line with paper cases.

2 Using electric beaters, beat the butter and sugar in a small mixing bowl until light and fluffy. Add the eggs, one at a time, beating after each addition. Add the essence and juice, beating until combined.

3 Transfer the mixture to a large bowl. Using a metal spoon, fold in the sifted flour alternately with the milk. Stir until just combined and the mixture is almost smooth.

4 Spoon level tablespoonfuls of the mixture into the paper cases. Bake for 10–15 minutes or until a skewer inserted in the centre of a cake comes out clean. Leave in tin for 5 minutes, then turn out onto a wire rack to cool completely.

5 Line tins again with patty cases and repeat the cooking procedure with remaining mixture to make a total of 36 cakes.

6 When the cupcakes are cold, carefully cut a round from the top of each one, cutting down to a depth of about 2 cm to allow for the filling.

7 Spoon a little jam into each cupcake. Top with 1 teaspoon of cream and dust with sifted icing sugar to serve.

LOW-FAT CHOCOLATE CUPCAKES

MAKES 12

3 eggs

185 g (6½ oz/1 cup) soft brown sugar

40 g (1½ oz) unsalted butter, melted

170 ml (5½ fl oz/⅔ cup) ready-made apple sauce

60 ml (2 fl oz/¼ cup) low-fat milk

85 g (3 oz/⅔ cup) unsweetened cocoa powder

185 g (6½ oz/1½ cups) self-raising flour

CHOCOLATE ICING (FROSTING)

125 g (4½ oz/1 cup) icing (confectioners') sugar, sifted

2 tablespoons unsweetened cocoa powder

1–2 tablespoons low-fat milk

1 **Preheat oven** to 180°C (350°F/Gas 4). Prepare a 12-hole cupcake tin with melted butter, dust lightly with flour and shake out any excess. Alternatively, use paper cases.

2 **Whisk the eggs** and sugar in a bowl for 5 minutes, or until pale and thick. Combine the butter, apple sauce and milk in a small bowl, stirring to mix well, then fold into the egg mixture. Sift the cocoa powder and flour together into a bowl, then fold into the egg mixture.

3 **Pour mixture** into the tin and bake for about 25 minutes, or until a skewer inserted in the centre of a cake comes out clean. Leave to cool in the tin for 5 minutes, then turn out onto a wire rack to cool completely.

4 **To make the chocolate icing,** combine the icing sugar and cocoa powder in a bowl, then stir in enough milk to form a thick paste. Stand the bowl over a saucepan of simmering water, stirring until the icing is smooth, then remove from the heat. Spread the icing over the cupcakes and leave to set.

WALNUT CUPCAKES WITH CHOCOLATE ICING

MAKES 12

185 g (6 oz) unsalted butter, softened

95 g (3¼ oz/½ cup) soft brown sugar

2 eggs

185 g (6½ oz/1½ cups) self-raising flour

90 g (3¼ oz/¾ cup) chopped walnuts

60 ml (2 fl oz/¼ cup) milk

CHOCOLATE ICING (FROSTING)

20 g (¾ oz) unsalted butter

125 g (4 oz) good-quality dark
    chocolate, chopped

chocolate sprinkles, to garnish

1 Preheat the oven to 180°C (350°F/ Gas 4). Prepare a 12-hole cupcake tin and line with paper cases.

2 Using electric beaters, beat the butter and sugar in a large mixing bowl for 5 minutes, or until thick and creamy. Add the eggs one at a time, beating well after each addition.

3 Using a metal spoon, fold in the sifted flour and 60 g (2 oz/½ cup) of walnuts alternately with the milk until just combined. Spoon mixture into the prepared tin and smooth the surface. Bake for 25 minutes, or until a skewer comes out clean when inserted in the centre of a cake. Remove from the oven and leave the cupcakes in the tin for 5 minutes before turning out onto a wire rack to completely cool.

4 To make the icing (frosting), place the butter and chocolate in a heatproof bowl. Bring a saucepan of water to the boil, then reduce the heat to a gentle simmer. Sit the bowl over the saucepan, making sure the base of the bowl does not touch the water. Stir occasionally until melted and smooth. Remove from the heat and leave to cool slightly. Spread the icing over the cupcakes with a flat-bladed knife. Garnish with chocolate sprinkles.

BRAN AND PRUNE CUPCAKES

MAKES 18

100 g (3½ oz/1½ cups) All-bran cereal
250 ml (9 fl oz/1 cup) milk
125 g (4½ oz/½ cup) chopped, pitted prunes
185 g (6½ oz/1½ cups) plain (all-purpose) flour
3 teaspoons baking powder
pinch of salt
95 g (3¼ oz/½ cup) dark brown sugar
1 egg
185 ml (6 fl oz/¾ cup) safflower or maize oil

1 **Preheat the oven** to 200°C (400°F/Gas 6). Prepare an 18-hole cupcake tin and insert paper cases.

2 **Combine cereal,** milk and prunes in a small mixing bowl and leave for 2 minutes.

3 **Sift together the flour,** baking powder and salt, then stir in sugar.

4 **Add the egg** and oil to the cereal mixture and beat well.

5 **Add the flour** mixture to the wet cereal mixture and stir until just combined—don't overmix, it should be lumpy

6 **Divide the mixture evenly** into the cupcake paper cases. Bake for 15–20 minutes or until a skewer inserted in the centre of a cake comes out clean. Leave in the tin for 5 minutes, then turn out onto a wire rack to cool completely.

RUM AND RAISIN CUPCAKES

SERVES 8

160 g (5½ oz/1 cup) raisins

60 ml (2 fl oz/¼ cup) dark rum

185 g (6 oz/1½ cups) self-raising flour

150 g (5½ oz) unsalted butter, chopped

140 g (4½ oz/¾ cup) soft brown sugar

3 eggs, lightly beaten

ice cream, to serve

1 Preheat the oven to 180°C (350°F/ Gas 4). Prepare an 8-hole cupcake tin and line with paper cases. Soak the raisins and rum in a small bowl for 10 minutes. Sift the flour into a large mixing bowl and make a well in the centre.

2 Melt the butter and sugar in a small saucepan over low heat, stirring until the sugar has dissolved. Remove from the heat. Combine with the rum and raisin mixture and add to the flour with the egg. Stir, making sure not to overmix, with a wooden spoon until just combined.

3 Divide the mixture evenly into the tins and smooth the surface. Bake for 20–25 minutes, or until a skewer comes out clean when inserted in the centre of a cake. Leave in tins for 5 minutes, then turn onto a wire rack to cool completely. Serve with ice cream.

MOIST JAM CUPCAKES

MAKES 8

125 g (4½ oz/1 cup) self-raising flour

30 g (1 oz/¼ cup) plain (all-purpose) flour

¼ teaspoon bicarbonate of soda (baking soda)

30 g (1 oz/¼ cup) cocoa powder

100 g (3½ oz) unsalted butter

95 g (3¼ oz/⅔ cup) soft brown sugar

105 g (3½ oz) jam (any flavour)

80 ml (2½ fl oz) hot water

2 eggs, lightly beaten

1 tablespoon jam, extra

whipped cream, to serve

1 **Preheat the oven** to 170°C (325°F/Gas 3). Prepare a 8-hole (large) cupcake tin and line with paper cases.

2 **Sift the flours,** bicarbonate of soda and cocoa into a large mixing bowl. Make a well in the centre.

3 **Combine the butter,** sugar, jam and water in a small pan. Stir over a low heat until butter has melted and sugar has dissolved, remove from heat.

4 **Add butter mixture** and eggs to dry ingredients. Stir with a wooden spoon until just combined (do not overbeat — the mixture should be lumpy).

5 **Pour the mixture** into the prepared cupcake tin. Bake for about 25 minutes or until a skewer comes out clean when inserted in the centre of a cake.

6 **Stand the cupcakes** in the tin for 15 minutes before turning out onto a wire rack to cool completely. Remove from paper cases.

7 **Heat the extra jam** in a small pan. Brush the hot jam on top of the cupcakes. Serve with whipped cream.

HONEY COCONUT CUPCAKES

MAKES 12

125 g (4 oz) unsalted butter, softened

140 g (4½ oz/⅔ cup) raw (demerara) sugar

2 large eggs, lightly beaten

1 teaspoon natural vanilla extract

90 g (3 oz/¼ cup) honey

45 g (1½ oz/½ cup) desiccated coconut

220 g (7 oz/1¾ cups) self-raising flour

1 teaspoon ground nutmeg

¼ teaspoon ground cinnamon

¼ teaspoon ground allspice

125 ml (4 fl oz/½ cup) milk

extra ground nutmeg, to decorate

HONEY AND CREAM CHEESE ICING (FROSTING)

125 g (4 oz) cream cheese, softened

60 g (2 oz/½ cup) icing (confectioners') sugar

1 tablespoon honey

1 **Preheat the oven** to 180°C (350°F/ Gas 4). Lightly grease a 12-hole cupcake tray and line with paper cases. Using electric beaters, beat the butter and sugar in a small mixing bowl until light and creamy Add the eggs gradually, beating thoroughly after each addition. Add the vanilla extract and honey. Beat until well combined.

2 **Transfer the mixture** to a large mixing bowl and add the desiccated coconut. Using a metal spoon, fold in sifted flour and spices alternating with milk. Stir until just combined and the mixture is almost smooth. Spoon into the prepared tin and smooth the surface.

3 **Bake for 30-35 minutes**, or until the skewer comes out clean when inserted in the centre of a cake. Leave the cakes in the tin for 10 minutes before turning out onto a wire rack to cool completely. Remove the baking paper.

4 **To make the icing (frosting),** beat the softened cream cheese with electric beaters in a small mixing bowl until creamy. Add the sifted icing sugar and honey, beating for 3 minutes, or until the mixture is smooth. Spread the icing evenly over the cake using a flat-bladed knife. Sprinkle the extra nutmeg over the top.

Note: The cake can be stored for 4 days in an airtight container.

PINEAPPLE AND PECAN CUPCAKES

MAKES 12

80 g (2¾ oz) unsalted butter, softened

250 g (9 oz/1 cup) sugar

2 eggs, lightly beaten

185 g (6½ oz/1½ cups) plain (all-purpose) flour

1¾ teaspoons baking powder

40 g (1½ oz/⅓ cup) finely chopped pecans, toasted

180 g (6 oz/¾ cup) finely chopped glacé pineapple

170 ml (5½ fl oz/⅔ cup) milk

icing (confectioners') sugar, to dust

1 **Preheat the oven** to 180°C (350°F/Gas 4). Lightly grease a 12-hole standard cupcake tray, or use paper cases. Beat the butter and sugar with electric beaters until combined. Add the egg and beat until pale and creamy.

2 **Sift together the flour,** baking powder and ¼ teaspoon salt. Add to the butter mixture with the pecans, pineapple and milk, then beat on low for 1 minute, or until almost smooth.

3 **Spoon the mixture** evenly into the prepared tin and smooth the surface. Bake for 20–25 minutes, or until a skewer comes out clean when inserted in the centre of a cake. Leave in the tin for 10 minutes before turning onto a wire rack to cool. If desired, dust with icing sugar just before serving.

Note: Glacé pineapple is available from health food stores and delicatessens.

VANILLA COCONUT CUPCAKES

MAKES 12

150 g (5½ oz) unsalted butter, cut into cubes

115 g (4 oz/½ cup) caster (superfine) sugar

2 teaspoons natural vanilla extract

2 eggs

185 g (6½ oz/1½ cups) plain (all-purpose) flour

1 teaspoon baking powder

45 g (1½ oz/½ cup) desiccated coconut

125 ml (4 fl oz/½ cup) milk

VANILLA ICING (FROSTING)

60 g (2¼ oz/1 cup) flaked coconut

20 g (¾ oz) unsalted butter, cut into cubes

2 teaspoons natural vanilla extract

185 g (6½ oz/1½ cups) icing (confectioners') sugar, sifted

1   **Preheat oven** to 180°C (350°F/Gas 4). Line 12 standard muffin holes with paper cases.

2   **Put the butter,** sugar and vanilla extract in a bowl and beat using electric beaters for 5 minutes, or until thick and creamy. Add the eggs, one at a time, and beat until well combined.

3   **Sift together the flour** and baking powder. Add to the mixture gradually. Stir in the desiccated coconut and the milk Put spoonfuls evenly into the paper cases.

4   **Bake for 18-20 minutes,** or until golden brown. Leave in the tin for 10 minutes. Cool on a wire rack.

5   **To make the vanilla icing (frosting),** spread the flaked coconut on a tray and lightly toast for 2–3 minutes in the oven. Take care that it doesn't burn. Put the butter in a small bowl and pour over 2 teaspoons of hot water to soften the butter. Add the vanilla extract. Put the icing sugar in a bowl, add the butter mixture and mix until smooth, adding a little more water if needed.

6   **Use a small spatula** to spread the cakes with the icing and dip each into the coconut flakes.

CHOCOLATE, GINGER AND FIG CUPCAKES

MAKES 8

125 g (4½ oz) unsalted butter, softened

230 g (8 oz/1 cup) firmly packed soft brown sugar

2 eggs, lightly beaten

185 g (6½ oz/1½ cups) self-raising flour

40 g (1¼ oz/⅓ cup) cocoa powder

185 ml (6 fl oz/¾ cup) milk

125 g (4½ oz/⅔ cup) dried figs, chopped

75 g (2½ oz/¼ cup) glacé ginger, chopped

1 **Preheat the oven** to 180°C (350°F/Gas 4). Brush an 8-cup cupcake tin with melted butter or oil. Using electric beaters, beat the butter and sugar in a mixing bowl until pale and creamy.

2 **Gradually add the egg,** beating well after each addition. Stir in the sifted flour and cocoa alternately with the milk to make a smooth batter. Fold in the figs and half the ginger.

3 **Spoon the mixture** evenly into the tin and smooth the surface. Scatter the remaining ginger over the top of the cakes. Bake for 25–30 minutes, or until a skewer comes out clean when inserted in the centre of a cake. Leave to cool in the tin for 5 minutes before turning out onto a wire rack to cool.

BUTTERFLY CUPCAKES

MAKES 12

120 g (4¼ oz) unsalted butter, softened

145 g (5½ oz/⅔ cup) caster (superfine) sugar

185 g (6½ oz/1½ cups) self-raising flour

125 ml (4 fl oz/½ cup) milk

2 teaspoons natural vanilla extract

2 eggs

125 ml (4 fl oz/½ cup) thick (double/heavy) cream

100 g (4 oz/⅓ cup) strawberry jam

icing (confectioners') sugar, to dust

1 **Preheat the oven** to 180°C (350°F/Gas 4). Line a 12-hole shallow patty pan or mini muffin tin with paper cases.

2 **Put the butter,** sugar, flour, milk, vanilla and eggs in a bowl and beat, using electric beaters on low speed for 2 minutes, or until well mixed. Increase the speed and beat for 2 minutes, or until smooth and pale.

3 **Divide the mixture** evenly among the cases and bake for 20 minutes, or until cooked and golden. Transfer to a wire rack to cool completely.

4 **Whip the cream to soft peaks.** Using a small sharp knife, cut shallow rounds from the top of each cake. Cut these in half. Spoon ½ tablespoon of the cream into the cavity in each cake, then top with 1 teaspoon of the jam. Position two halves of the cake tops in the jam in each cake to resemble butterfly wings. Dust the cakes with icing sugar before serving.

Note: To make iced cup cakes, don't cut off the tops. Mix 60 g (2¼ oz/½ cup) sifted icing (confectioners') sugar, 1 teaspoon softened unsalted butter, ½ teaspoon natural vanilla extract and up to 3 teaspoons hot water to form a smooth paste, then spread the icing (frosting) on the cooled cakes.

RHUBARB CUPCAKES

MAKES 12

150 g (5½ oz/1¼ cups) finely sliced fresh rhubarb

310 g (11 oz/2½ cups) self-raising flour, sifted

250 g (9 oz/1 cup) caster (superfine) sugar

1 teaspoon natural vanilla extract

2 eggs, lightly beaten

125 g (3¼ oz/½ cup) plain yoghurt

1 tablespoon rosewater

125 g (4½ oz) unsalted butter, melted

plain yoghurt or whipped cream, to serve

1 **Preheat the oven** to 180°C (350°F/Gas 4). Lightly grease a 12-hole cupcake tray and line with paper cases.

2 **Combine the rhubarb,** flour and sugar in a bowl.

3 **Add the vanilla extract,** egg, yoghurt, rosewater and melted butter, stirring until the mixture is just combined.

4 **Spoon the mixture** into the cupcake tin and bake for 35 to 40 minutes, or until a skewer comes out clean when inserted in the centre of a cake. Leave in tin for 10 minutes before turning out onto a wire rack. Serve with yoghurt or cream, if desired.

CLASSIC CUPCAKES WITH ICING

MAKES 18

250 g (9 oz/2 cups) self-raising flour

165 g (5¾ oz/¾ cup) sugar

125 g (4½ oz) unsalted butter, softened

3 eggs

3 tablespoons milk

½ teaspoon natural vanilla extract

CARAMEL ICING (FROSTING)

185 g (6½ oz/1½ cups) icing
    (confectioners') sugar

1 tablespoon milk

2 tablespoons golden syrup or honey

30 g (1 oz) unsalted butter, softened

1 **Preheat the oven** to 180°C (350°F/Gas 4). Line 18 standard muffin holes with paper cases.

2 **Sift the flour** and sugar into a bowl. Add the butter, eggs, milk and vanilla and beat until smooth. Fill the paper cases three-quarters full with the mixture.

3 **Bake for 15 minutes,** or until lightly golden. Cool on a wire rack.

4 **To make the icing (frosting),** put the icing sugar, milk, golden syrup and butter in a bowl and beat with a wooden spoon until smooth. Spread over each cake with a flat-bladed knife.

SPICED CHRISTMAS CUPCAKES

MAKES 12

325 g (1½ oz) mixed dried fruit

80 ml (2½ fl oz/⅓ cup) rum or brandy

310 g (11 oz/2½ cups) self-raising flour

1 teaspoons mixed (pumpkin pie) spice

1 teaspoon ground cinnamon

½ teaspoon ground nutmeg

155 g (5½ oz/⅔ cup) firmly packed soft
    brown sugar

125 ml (4 fl oz/½ cup) milk

1 egg, lightly beaten

2 tablespoons apricot jam

½ teaspoon very finely grated
    lemon zest

½ teaspoon very finely grated
    orange zest

125 g (4½ oz) unsalted butter,
    melted and cooled

icing (confectioners') sugar, to dust

125 g (4½ oz) ready-made icing

2 tablespoons apricot jam, extra,
    warmed and sieved

red glacé cherries, for decoration

angelica, for decoration

1 **Combine the mixed dried fruit** and rum in a large bowl. Cover and leave to marinate, stirring frequently, for 1–2 hours, or until the rum has been completely absorbed by the fruit.

2 **Preheat the oven** to 200°C (400°F/Gas 6). Line a 12-hole standard muffin tin with paper cases. Sift the flour, mixed spice, cinnamon and nutmeg into a large bowl and stir in the brown sugar. Make a well in the centre.

3 **Put the milk,** egg, apricot jam, lemon and orange zest and melted butter in a bowl, mix together and pour into the well in the dry ingredients. Stir in the marinated dried fruit mixture. Fold gently until just combined — the batter should be lumpy.

4 **Divide the mixture** evenly among the muffin holes. Bake for 20 minutes, or until a skewer inserted in the middle of a cake comes out clean. Cool in the tins for 5 minutes, then transfer the cakes to a wire rack to cool completely.

5 **To make the icing (frosting),** place the ready-made icing on a work surface dusted with a little icing sugar. Roll out to a thickness of about 2 mm (¹⁄₁₆ inch) and, using a 7 cm (2¾ inch) fluted round cutter, cut out 12 rounds from the icing. Reroll the scraps of icing if necessary.

6 **Brush the tops** of the cooled cakes lightly with the extra apricot jam and place a round of icing on top of each cake. Decorate with whole or halved red glacé cherries.

SLICES

CHOCOLATE TRUFFLE MACAROON SLICE

MAKES 24

3 egg whites

185 g (6½ oz/¾ cup) caster (superfine) sugar

180 g (6 oz/2 cups) desiccated coconut

250 g (9 oz) dark chocolate

300 ml (10½ fl oz/1¼ cups) thick (double/heavy) cream

1 tablespoon cocoa powder

1 **Preheat the oven** to 180°C (350°F/Gas 4). Lightly grease a 20 x 30 cm (8 x 12 inch) shallow baking tin and line with baking paper, leaving it hanging over the two long sides.

2 **Beat the egg whites** in a clean, dry bowl until soft peaks form. Slowly add the sugar, beating well after each addition until stiff and glossy. Fold in the coconut. Spread mixture into the tin and bake for 20 minutes, or until light brown. While still warm, press down lightly but firmly with a palette knife. Leave to cool completely.

3 **Chop the chocolate** into small even-sized pieces and place in a heatproof bowl. Bring a saucepan of water to the boil, then remove from the heat. Sit the bowl over the pan — ensure the bowl doesn't touch the water. Stand, stirring occasionally, until the chocolate has melted. Cool slightly.

4 **Beat the cream** until thick. Gently fold in the chocolate until well combined — do not overmix or it will curdle. Spread evenly over the base and refrigerate for 3 hours, or until set. Lift from the tin and dust with the cocoa.

WALNUT BROWNIES

MAKES 20

100 g (3½ oz) unsalted butter

125 g (4½ oz/⅔ cup) lightly packed soft brown sugar

40 g (1½ oz/⅓ cup) sultanas (golden raisins), chopped

125 g (4½ oz/1 cup) self-raising flour

125 g (4½ oz/1 cup) plain (all-purpose) flour

1 teaspoon ground cinnamon

1 tablespoon unsweetened cocoa powder

60 g (2¼ oz/½ cup) chopped walnuts

90 g (3¼ oz) chocolate chips

20 walnut halves

ICING (FROSTING)

60 g (2¼ oz) unsalted butter

90 g (3¼ oz/¾ cup) icing (confectioners') sugar

1 tablespoon unsweetened cocoa powder

1 tablespoon milk

1 **Preheat the oven** to 180°C (350°F/Gas 4). Lightly grease a 27 x 18 cm (10¾ x 7 inch) shallow rectangular baking tin. Line the base with baking paper, extending it over the two longer sides. Grease the paper.

2 **Combine butter,** sugar, sultanas and 185 ml (6 fl oz/¾ cup) water in a small saucepan. Constantly stir over low heat for 5 minutes, or until the butter is melted and the sugar is dissolved. Remove from the heat.

3 **Sift the dry ingredients** into a large mixing bowl. Add the chopped nuts and chocolate chips. Make a well in the centre of the dry ingredients and add the butter mixture. Using a wooden spoon, stir until just combined. Do not overmix.

4 **Spoon the mixture** into the prepared tin and smooth the surface. Bake for 25–30 minutes, or until a skewer comes out clean when inserted in the centre of the slice. Leave in the tin for 20 minutes before turning onto a wire rack to cool completely.

5 **To make the icing** (frosting), beat the butter with electric beaters until light and creamy. Add the icing sugar, cocoa and milk. Beat until smooth. Spread the icing over the brownie. Cut into diamonds and top with the walnut halves.

APRICOT AND MACAROON SLICE

MAKES 16

100 g (3½ oz) unsalted butter, softened

90 g (¼ oz/⅓ cup) caster (superfine) sugar

1 egg

185 g (6½ oz/1½ cups) plain (all-purpose) flour

½ teaspoon baking powder

FILLING

250 g (9 oz/1⅓ cups) dried apricots, roughly chopped

1 tablespoon Grand Marnier

2 tablespoons caster (superfine) sugar

TOPPING

100 g (3¼ oz/3½ oz) unsalted butter

90 g (⅓ cup) caster (superfine) sugar

1 teaspoon natural vanilla extract

2 eggs

270 g (9½ oz/3 cups) desiccated coconut

40 g (1½ oz/⅓ cup) plain (all-purpose) flour

½ teaspoon baking powder

1 Preheat the oven to 180°C (350°F/Gas 4). Lightly grease a 20 x 30 cm (8 x 12 inch) baking tin and line with baking paper. Cream the butter and sugar until light and fluffy. Add the egg and beat well. Sift the flour and baking powder and fold into the butter mixture with a metal spoon. Press firmly into the tin and bake for 20 to 25 minutes, or until golden brown. Cool.

2 To make the filling, combine the apricots, Grand Marnier, sugar and 125 ml (4 fl oz/½ cup) boiling water in a bowl. Set aside for 30 minutes, then purée in a food processor. Spread evenly over the cooled base.

3 To make the topping, cream the butter, sugar and vanilla until light and fluffy. Gradually add the eggs, beating well after each addition. Fold in the coconut, flour and baking powder with a large metal spoon. Spoon onto the apricot leaving it lumpy and loose — do not press down. Bake for 20 to 25 minutes, or until lightly golden.

PEPPERMINT AND CHOCOLATE SLICE

MAKES 20

220 g (7¾ oz/1¾ cups) plain (all-purpose) flour
1 teaspoon baking powder
95 g (3¼ oz/½ cup) soft brown sugar
180 g (6 oz) unsalted butter, melted
60 g (2¼ oz) Copha (white vegetable shortening)
435 g (3½ cups) icing (confectioners') sugar, sifted
1 teaspoon peppermint extract
2 tablespoons milk
2 tablespoons cream
300 g (10½ oz) dark cooking chocolate
70 g (2½ oz) unsalted butter, extra

1 **Preheat the oven** to 180°C (350°F/Gas 4). Grease a 20 x 30 cm (8 x 12 inch) baking tin and line with baking paper, leaving the paper hanging over the two long sides of the tin.

2 **Sift together** the flour and baking powder and add the brown sugar. Stir in the melted butter, press into the tin and bake for 20 minutes. Cool.

3 **Melt the Copha** in a saucepan over medium heat. Stir in the icing sugar, peppermint extract, milk and cream. Mix well and pour over the pastry base. Leave to set.

4 **Chop the chocolate** and extra butter into small even-sized pieces and place in a heatproof bowl. Bring a saucepan of water to the boil and remove from the heat. Sit the bowl over the pan, making sure the bowl doesn't touch the water. Stand, stirring occasionally, until melted and combined. Cool slightly, then spread over the icing. Chill until set, then cut into pieces.

RASPBERRY AND COCONUT SLICE

MAKES 30

280 g (10 oz/2¼ cups) plain
(all-purpose) flour

3 tablespoons ground almonds

500 g (1 lb 2 oz/2 cups) caster
(superfine) sugar

250 g (9 oz) unsalted butter, chilled

½ teaspoon ground nutmeg

½ teaspoon baking powder

4 eggs

1 teaspoon natural vanilla extract

1 tablespoon lemon juice

300 g (10½ oz/2½ cups) fresh or
thawed frozen raspberries

90 g (3¼ oz/1 cup) desiccated coconut

icing (confectioners') sugar, to dust

1 **Preheat the oven** to 180°C (350°F/Gas 4). Lightly grease a 20 x 30 cm (8 x 12 inch) shallow tin and line with baking paper, hanging over the two long sides.

2 **Sift 220 g** (7¾ oz/1¾ cups) of the flour into a bowl. Add the ground almonds and 125 g (4½ oz/½ cup) of the caster sugar and stir to combine. Rub the butter into the flour with your fingertips until it resembles fine breadcrumbs. Press the mixture into the tin and bake for 20 to 25 minutes, or until golden. Reduce the oven to 150°C (300°F/Gas 2).

3 **Sift the nutmeg,** baking powder and the remaining flour onto a piece of baking paper. Beat the eggs, vanilla and remaining sugar with electric beaters for 4 minutes, or until light and fluffy. Fold in the flour with a large metal spoon. Stir in the lemon juice, raspberries and coconut and pour over the base.

4 **Bake for 1 hour,** or until golden and firm. Chill in the tin, then cut into pieces. Dust with icing sugar.

COCONUT AND PINEAPPLE SLICE

MAKES 24

20 g (¾ oz/⅓ cup) shredded coconut

90 g (3¼ oz/¾ cup) self-raising flour

50 g (1¾ oz/½ cup) plain (all-purpose) flour

140 g (5 oz/¾ cup) soft brown sugar

2 tablespoons sunflower seeds

2 tablespoons sesame seeds

70 g (2½ oz/½ cup) chopped macadamia nuts

60 g (2¼ oz/⅓ cup) chopped dates

1 tablespoon chopped glacé ginger

45 g (1½ oz/½ cup) desiccated coconut

230 g tin crushed pineapple, drained

100 g (3½ oz) unsalted butter, melted

2 eggs, lightly beaten

ICING (FROSTING)

250 g (9 oz/2 cups) icing (confectioners') sugar

30 g (1 oz) unsalted butter, melted

1½ tablespoons lemon juice

1   **Preheat the oven** to 170°C (325°F/Gas 3). Spread the coconut evenly on a baking tray and toast for 5 to 8 minutes, or until lightly golden. Grease a 20 x 30 cm (8 x 12 inch) shallow baking tin and line with enough baking paper to overlap on the longer sides — this will make the slice easier to remove once baked.

2   **Sift the self-raising** and plain flours into a large bowl. Add the brown sugar, seeds, macadamia nuts, dates, ginger and desiccated coconut. Stir in the pineapple, melted butter and beaten egg, and mix well.

3   **Spoon the mixture** into the prepared tin. Bake for 25 to 30 minutes, or until golden brown. Cool in the tin, remove and cover with the icing.

4   **To make the icing,** combine the icing sugar, melted butter and lemon juice in a small bowl. Stir in 1–2 teaspoons of boiling water to reach a smooth consistency. Spread evenly over the slice. Sprinkle the top with the toasted shredded coconut and when set, slice and serve.

Note: Use other nuts or seeds, such as pumpkin seeds or almonds, if desired.

VANILLA SLICE

MAKES 9

500 g (1 lb 2 oz) ready-made puff pastry

250 g (9 oz/1 cup) caster (superfine) sugar

90 g (3¼ oz/¾ cup) cornflour (cornstarch)

60 g (2¼ oz/½ cup) custard powder

1 litre (35 fl oz/4 cups) cream

60 g (2¼ oz) unsalted butter, cubed

2 teaspoons natural vanilla extract

3 egg yolks

ICING (FROSTING)

185 g (6½ oz/1½ cups) icing (confectioners') sugar

60 g (2¼ oz/¼ cup) passionfruit pulp

15 g (½ oz) unsalted butter, melted

1   Preheat the oven to 210°C (415°F/Gas 6–7). Lightly grease two baking trays with oil. Line the base and sides of a shallow 23 cm (9 inch) square cake tin with foil, leaving the foil hanging over two opposite sides.

2   Divide the pastry in half, roll each piece to a 25 cm (10 inch) square 3 mm (⅛ inch) thick and put on a baking tray. Prick all over with a fork and bake for 8 minutes, or until golden. Trim each pastry sheet to a 23 cm (9 inch) square. Put one sheet top side down in the cake tin.

3   Combine the sugar, cornflour and custard powder in a saucepan. Add the cream, stirring constantly over medium heat for 2 minutes, or until it boils and thickens. Add the butter and vanilla and stir until smooth. Remove from the heat and whisk in the egg yolks until combined. Spread the custard over the pastry in the tin, then cover with the other pastry sheet, top side down. Cool completely.

4   To make the icing, combine the icing sugar, passionfruit pulp and butter in a bowl, and stir until smooth.

5   Lift the slice out of the tin using the foil as handles. Ice the top and leave to set before cutting with a serrated knife.

CHOCOLATE AND CARAMEL SLICE

MAKES 24

200 g (7 oz) plain chocolate biscuits, crushed

100 g (3½ oz) unsalted butter, melted

2 tablespoons desiccated coconut

125 g (4½ oz) unsalted butter, extra

400 ml (14 fl oz) tin sweetened condensed milk

90 g (13¼ oz/⅓ cup) caster (superfine) sugar

3 tablespoons maple syrup

250 g (9 oz) dark chocolate

2 teaspoons oil

1 Grease a 30 x 20 cm (12 in x 8 in) shallow baking tin. Line with baking paper, leaving it hanging over the two long sides.

2 **Combine the biscuits,** melted butter and coconut in a bowl, then press into the tin and smooth the surface.

3 **Combine the butter,** condensed milk, sugar and maple syrup in a small saucepan. Stir over low heat for 15 minutes, or until the sugar has dissolved and the mixture is smooth, thick and lightly coloured. Remove from the heat and cool slightly. Pour over the biscuit base and smooth the surface. Refrigerate for 30 minutes, or until firm.

4 Chop the chocolate into small even-sized pieces and place in a heatproof bowl. Bring a saucepan of water to the boil and remove from the heat. Sit the bowl over the saucepan, making sure the bowl doesn't touch the water. Allow to stand, stirring occasionally, until the chocolate has melted. Add the oil and stir until smooth. Spread over the caramel and leave until partially set before marking into 24 triangles. Refrigerate until firm. Cut into triangles before serving.

POPPY SEED SLICE

MAKES 14

135 g (4¾ oz/1 cup) plain (all-purpose) flour

75 g (2½ oz) unsalted butter, chilled and chopped

60 g (2¼ oz/¼ cup) caster (superfine) sugar

1 egg yolk

40 g (1½ oz/¼ cup) poppy seeds

2 tablespoons milk, warmed

125 g (4½ oz) unsalted butter, extra

90 g (3¼ oz/⅓ cup) caster (superfine) sugar, extra

1 teaspoon finely grated lemon zest

1 egg

90 g (3¼ oz/¾ cup) plain (all-purpose) flour, extra, sifted

125 g (4½ oz/1 cup) icing (confectioners') sugar

½ teaspoon finely grated lemon zest, extra

1 tablespoon lemon juice

1   **Preheat the oven** to 180°C (350°F/Gas 4). Grease an 11 x 35 cm (4¼ x 14 inch) loose-based flan tin. Sift the flour into a bowl and rub in the butter with your fingers until it resembles breadcrumbs. Stir in the sugar. Make a well in the centre and add 2–3 teaspoons water and the egg yolk. Mix with a flat-bladed knife, using a cutting action until it comes together in beads. Press into a ball and flatten slightly. Cover in plastic wrap and chill for 15 minutes.

2   **Roll out the dough** to fit the base and sides of the tin. Trim the edges. Blind bake the pastry for 10 minutes, then remove the paper and beads and bake for 5 minutes, or until the pastry is dry. Cool.

3   **Soak the poppy seeds** in the milk for 10 minutes. Beat the extra butter and sugar and the zest until light and fluffy. Beat in the egg and stir in the poppy seed mixture and extra flour. Spread over the pastry and bake for 25 minutes, or until light brown and cooked through. Cool in the tin until just warm.

4   **Combine the icing sugar**, extra zest and enough juice to form a paste. Spread over the slice and cool.

STRAWBERRY AND MASCARPONE SLICE

MAKES 24

175 g (6 oz) unsalted butter, softened

70 g (2½ oz/⅓ cup) caster (superfine) sugar

1 egg yolk

250 g (9 oz/2 cups) plain (all-purpose) flour, sifted

300 g (10½ oz/1⅓ cups) mascarpone cheese

60 g (2¼ oz/½ cup) icing (confectioners') sugar, sifted

1 tablespoon lemon juice

300 g (10½ oz/2 cups) strawberries, cut into quarters

50 g (1¾ oz) dark chocolate

1 **Preheat the oven** to 180°C (350°F/Gas 4). Lightly grease a 20 x 30 cm (8 x 12 inch) shallow baking tin and line with baking paper, leaving it hanging over the two long sides.

2 **Beat the butter** and sugar with electric beaters until light and fluffy. Add the egg yolk and beat well. Fold in the sifted flour until well combined. Press firmly into the prepared baking tin and prick all over with a fork. Bake for 25 minutes, or until light brown. Cool completely.

3 **Beat the mascarpone,** icing sugar and juice with a wooden spoon until smooth. Stir in the strawberries. Spoon over the base and refrigerate for 3 hours, or until firm.

4 **Chop the chocolate** into small even-sized pieces and place in a heatproof bowl. Bring a saucepan of water to the boil, then remove from the heat. Sit the bowl over the pan — ensure the bowl doesn't touch the water. Stand, stirring occasionally, until the chocolate has melted. Drizzle over the slice, then cut into pieces.

GINGER CHEESECAKE SLICE

MAKES 24

200 g (7 oz) ginger-flavoured biscuits (cookies), finely crushed

60 g (2¼ oz) unsalted butter, melted

½ teaspoon ground cinnamon

500 g (1 lb 2 oz/2 cups) cream cheese

125 ml (4 fl oz/½ cup) golden syrup

2 tablespoons caster (superfine) sugar

2 eggs, lightly beaten

55 g (2 oz/¼ cup) finely chopped crystallized ginger

125 ml (4 fl oz/½ cup) lightly whipped cream

125 ml (4 fl oz/½ cup) thick (double/ heavy) cream, extra

2 teaspoons caster (superfine) sugar, extra

55 g (2 oz/¼ cup) crystallized ginger, extra, thinly sliced

1 **Preheat the oven** to 170°C (325°F/Gas 3). Lightly grease a 20 x 30 cm (8 x 12 inch) baking tin and line with baking paper, leaving the paper hanging over the two long sides.

2 **Combine the biscuits,** butter and cinnamon and press into the base of the tin. Refrigerate for 30 minutes, or until firm.

3 **Beat the cream cheese,** golden syrup and sugar with electric beaters until light and fluffy. Add the eggs, one at a time, beating well after each addition. Fold in the ginger and lightly whipped cream. Spread over the base and bake for 25 minutes, or until just set. Turn off the oven and cool with the door slightly ajar.

4 **Remove from the tin** and trim the edges. Beat the extra cream and extra sugar until soft peaks form and spread over the cheesecake. Using a hot dry knife, cut into three strips lengthways and then cut each strip into eight pieces. Decorate with the extra ginger.

FIG AND CINNAMON SLICE

MAKES 15

125 g (4½ oz) unsalted butter, softened

55 g (2 oz/¼ cup) soft brown sugar, firmly packed

1 teaspoon ground cinnamon

185 g (6½ oz/1½ cups) plain (all-purpose) flour

375 g (13 oz/2⅓ cups) dried figs

1 cinnamon stick

125 g (4½ oz/½ cup) caster (superfine) sugar

1 **Preheat the oven** to 180°C (350°F/Gas 4). Lightly grease an 18 x 27 cm (7 x 10¾ inch) baking tin and line with baking paper, hanging over the two long sides.

2 **Beat the butter,** brown sugar and cinnamon until light and fluffy, then fold in the flour with a large metal spoon. Press the mixture evenly into the tin and bake for 25 minutes. Cool slightly.

3 **Combine the dried figs,** cinnamon stick, sugar and 375 ml (13 fl oz/1½ cups) boiling water in a saucepan and bring to the boil. Reduce the heat and simmer for 20 minutes, or until the figs have softened and the water has reduced by a third. Remove the cinnamon stick and place the mixture in a food processor. Process in short bursts until smooth.

4 **Pour onto the cooked base** and bake for 10 minutes, or until set. Cool in the tin, then lift out and cut into squares.

BERRY AND APPLE SLICE

MAKES 12

150 g (5½ oz) unsalted butter

320 g (11¼ oz/1⅓ cups) caster (superfine) sugar

2 eggs, lightly beaten

250 g (9 oz/2 cups) self-raising flour, sifted

160 ml (5¼ fl oz/⅔ cup) buttermilk

1 teaspoon natural vanilla extract

2 large apples

150 g (5½ oz/1 cup) blueberries

150 g (5½ oz/1¼ cups) blackberries

icing (confectioners') sugar, to dust

1 Preheat the oven to 180°C (350°F/Gas 4). Lightly grease a 30 x 20 cm (12 x 8 in) shallow baking tin and line with baking paper, leaving it hanging over the two long sides.

2 Beat the butter and sugar with electric beaters until light and fluffy. Add the egg gradually, beating well after each addition. Stir in the flour and buttermilk alternately and mix until smooth. Stir through the vanilla. Spread a 5 mm (¼ in) layer of mixture over the base of the tin.

3 Peel, quarter and core the apples. Cut into very thin slices and arrange on the mixture. Spoon the remaining mixture over the apple and smooth the surface, then scatter with the blueberries and blackberries. Bake on the middle rack for 40 minutes, or until cooked and golden.

4 Cool in the tin for 30 minutes before lifting onto a wire rack. When completely cooled, dust with icing sugar and cut into squares.

COCONUT PINEAPPLE SQUARES

MAKES 12

250 g (9 oz) oatmeal biscuits, crushed

90 g (3¼ oz/1½ cups) shredded coconut

250 g (9 oz) chopped glacé (candied) pineapple

90 g (3¼ oz/1 cup) flaked almonds

200 ml (7 fl oz) sweetened condensed milk

100 g (3½ oz) unsalted butter, melted

COCONUT ICING (FROSTING)

60 g (2¼ oz) unsalted butter, softened

few drops coconut essence

90 g (3¼ oz/¾ cup) icing (confectioners') sugar, sifted

1 tablespoon milk

90 g (3¼ oz) toasted flaked coconut (see Note)

1 **Preheat the oven** to 180°C (350°F/Gas 4). Lightly grease a shallow 27 x 18 cm (10¾ x 7 inch) rectangular baking tin and line with baking paper.

2 **Combine the crushed biscuits,** coconut, pineapple and almonds in a large mixing bowl. Make a well in the centre of the ingredients and pour in the condensed milk and butter. Stir until well combined.

3 **Press the mixture** firmly into the prepared tin. Bake for 20 minutes, or until the top is lightly golden. Leave to cool in the tin.

4 **To make the coconut icing** (frosting), beat the butter and coconut essence with electric beaters in a mixing bowl until light and creamy. Add icing sugar and milk. Beat until smooth and fluffy. Spread the icing evenly over the slice and sprinkle with the toasted coconut. Cut into squares.

Note: The slice may be stored for up to 3 days in an airtight container or up to 2 months in the freezer, without icing. Toast the coconut by simply spreading it on a baking tray and baking for 5 minutes, or until golden.

PLUM AND ALMOND SLICE

MAKES 9

165 g (5¾ oz) unsalted butter, cubed and softened

145 g (5½ oz/⅔ cup) caster (superfine) sugar

2 eggs

60 g (2¼ oz/½ cup) plain (all-purpose) flour

40 g (1½ oz/⅓ cup) cornflour (cornstarch)

2 tablespoons rice flour

1½ tablespoons thinly sliced glacé ginger

825 g (1 lb 13 oz) tinned plums in syrup, drained, seeded and halved

90 g (3¼ oz/1 cup) flaked almonds

1 tablespoon honey, warmed

1   Preheat the oven to 180°C (350°F/Gas 4). Lightly grease a 20 cm (8 inch) square tin and line with baking paper, leaving the paper hanging over the top edge of the tin on all sides. Cream butter and sugar in a small bowl using electric beaters until light and fluffy. Add the eggs one at a time, beating well after each addition. Sift the flours over the mixture and fold into the mixture with the ginger. Spread into the tin. Arrange the plum halves on top, pressing them in. Scatter with flaked almonds, pressing in gently, then drizzle with the honey.

2   Bake for 1 hour 10 minutes, or until firm and golden. Cover with foil if the slice starts to brown too much. Cool in the tin, then lift out, using the paper as handles, before cutting into pieces.

Note: The slice can be kept for up to 4 or 5 days if stored in an airtight container in the refrigerator.

CONTINENTAL SLICE

MAKES 36

125 g (4½ oz) unsalted butter

115 g (4 oz/½ cup) caster (superfine) sugar

30 g (1 oz/¼ cup) unsweetened cocoa powder

250 g (9 oz) shredded wheat biscuits, crushed

65 g (2½ oz/¾ cup) desiccated coconut

30 g (1 oz/¼ cup) chopped hazelnuts

60 g (2¼ oz/¼ cup) chopped glacé cherries

1 egg, lightly beaten

1 teaspoon natural vanilla extract

TOPPING

215 g (7¾ oz/1¾ cups) icing (confectioners') sugar

2 tablespoons custard powder or instant vanilla pudding mix

1 tablespoon Grand Marnier

60 g (2¼ oz) unsalted butter

125 g (4½ oz) dark chocolate

60 g (2¼ oz) Copha (white vegetable shortening)

1 Line the base and sides of an 18 x 28 cm (7 x 11¼ inch) shallow tin with foil. Combine the butter, sugar and cocoa powder in a small saucepan. Stir over low heat until the butter melts and the mixture is well combined. Cook, stirring, for 1 minute. Remove from the heat and cool slightly.

2 Combine the biscuit crumbs, coconut, hazelnuts and cherries in a large bowl. Make a well in the centre, then add the butter mixture, egg and vanilla all at once and stir well. Press the mixture firmly with the back of a spoon into the prepared tin. Refrigerate until firm.

3 To make the topping, combine the icing sugar with the custard powder. Mix the Grand Marnier with 1 tablespoon hot water. Beat the butter, using electric beaters, until creamy. Gradually add the sugar mixture and the Grand Marnier mixture, alternately, to the butter. Beat the mixture until light and creamy. Spread evenly over the base and then refrigerate until set.

4 Combine the chocolate and Copha in a heatproof bowl. Place the bowl over a saucepan of simmering water, making sure the base of the bowl does not touch the water, and stir over low heat until the chocolate melts and the mixture is smooth. Spread over the slice. Refrigerate for 4 hours or until firm. Cut the slice into squares to serve.

BAKEWELL SLICE

MAKES 15

125 g (4½ oz/1 cup) plain (all-purpose) flour

30 g (1 oz/¼ cup) icing (confectioners') sugar

170 g (6 oz) unsalted butter, chilled and chopped

1 egg yolk

125 g (4½ oz/½ cup) caster (superfine) sugar

4 eggs

125 g (4½ oz/1¼ cups) ground almonds

2 drops almond extract

160 g (5¾ oz/½ cup) raspberry jam

25 g (1 oz/¼ cup) flaked almonds

1   Preheat the oven to 180°C (350°F/Gas 4). Lightly grease a 20 x 30 cm (8 x 12 inch) baking tin and line with baking paper, hanging over the two long sides. Sift the flour and 1 tablespoon of the icing sugar into a bowl, add 50 g (1¾ oz) of the butter and rub it in until the mixture resembles breadcrumbs. Add the egg yolk and 2 tablespoons cold water and mix with a flat-bladed knife until the mixture comes together in beads. Gather into a ball, cover with plastic wrap and refrigerate for 30 minutes. Roll out between two sheets of baking paper, remove the paper and put in the tin, pressing into the edges. Bake for 10 minutes. Cool.

2   Beat the remaining butter and the caster sugar with electric beaters until creamy. Add the eggs and fold in the ground almonds and almond extract.

3   Spread the jam over the pastry base and pour over the filling. Sprinkle with almonds and bake for 30 to 35 minutes, or until firm. Allow to cool.

4   Sift the remaining icing sugar into a bowl and mix in 2–3 teaspoons warm water to form a free-flowing paste. Drizzle over the slice in a zigzag pattern and leave to set. Trim the edges and cut into squares.

PASSIONFRUIT AND COCONUT CHEESE SLICE

MAKES 24

100 g (3½ oz/¾ cup) slivered almonds

125 g (4½ oz/1 cup) plain (all-purpose) flour

1 teaspoon baking powder

100 g (3½ oz) unsalted butter, chopped

125 g (4½ oz/½ cup) caster (superfine) sugar

1 egg yolk

25 g (1 oz/¼ cup) desiccated coconut

750 g (1 lb 10 oz/3 cups) cream cheese, softened

2 eggs

185 ml (6 fl oz/¾ cup) coconut milk

3 teaspoons natural vanilla extract

½ teaspoon lemon juice

185 g (6½ oz/¾ cup) caster (superfine) sugar, extra

65 g (2¼ oz/¾ cup) flaked almonds, toasted

TOPPING

90 g (3¼ oz/¾ cup) icing (confectioners') sugar

40 g (1½ oz) unsalted butter, softened

1 tablespoon cornflour (cornstarch)

2 tablespoons strained passionfruit juice

1 **Finely chop the almonds** in a food processor. Sift the flour and baking powder into a bowl. Rub the butter into the flour until it resembles breadcrumbs. Stir in the almonds and sugar. Make a well in the centre and add the egg yolk. Mix with a flat-bladed knife until the mixture comes together in beads. Remove to a lightly floured work surface and shape into a ball. Flatten slightly, cover in plastic wrap and refrigerate for 30 minutes.

2 **Preheat the oven** to 170°C (325°F/Gas 3). Grease a 30 x 20 x 5 cm (12 x 8 x 2 inch) tin and line with baking paper, leaving it hanging over on the two long sides. Roll the dough out to fit the tin and press in evenly. Sprinkle with coconut and lightly press it in. Bake for 10 minutes. Cool for 10 minutes.

3 **Combine the cream cheese** and the eggs in the food processor. Add coconut milk, vanilla, lemon juice and the extra sugar, and blend until smooth. Pour over the base. Bake for 40 minutes. Cool in the tin.

4 **To make the topping,** mix the icing sugar and butter with a wooden spoon until smooth. Stir in the cornflour, then the passionfruit juice. Mix until smooth, then spread over the slice. Scatter over the toasted almonds. Leave to set, then cut into 5 cm (2 in) squares.

CHEWY NUT AND SEED SLICE

MAKES 18

100 g (3½ oz/⅔ cup) shelled pistachio nuts

200 g (7 oz) unsalted butter, chopped

160 g (5¾ oz/⅔ cup) caster (superfine) sugar

1 teaspoon natural vanilla extract

1 tablespoon finely grated orange zest

2 eggs

60 g (2¼ oz/½ cup) self-raising flour, sifted

125 ml (4 fl oz/½ cup) orange juice

185 g (6½ oz/1½ cups) fine semolina

250 g (9 oz/1 cup) caster (superfine) sugar, extra

125 ml (4 fl oz/½ cup) orange juice, extra

icing (confectioners') sugar, to dust

1 **Preheat the oven** to 180°C (350°F/Gas 4). Lightly grease a 20 x 30 cm (8 x 12 inch) shallow baking tin and line with baking paper, leaving it hanging over on the two long sides.

2 **Bake the pistachios** for 8–10 minutes, or until they are lightly toasted. Cool, then chop.

3 **Beat the butter and sugar** with electric beaters until light and fluffy. Add the vanilla, orange zest and eggs, and beat until combined.

4 **Add the flour,** orange juice, semolina and pistachio nuts, and fold in with a spatula until just combined — do not overmix. Spread mixture into the tin. Bake for 30 minutes, or until golden brown and firm when lightly touched. Cool for 10 minutes in the tin, then on a wire rack placed on a tray.

5 **Mix the extra sugar** and orange juice in a small saucepan. Bring to the boil over medium heat, then simmer for 1 minute. Spoon over the slice. Cool and cut into squares or diamonds. Dust with icing sugar.

PASSIONFRUIT AND LEMON DELICIOUS SLICE

MAKES 18

200 g (7 oz) unsalted butter

175 g (6 oz/½ cup) golden syrup

125 g (4½ oz/½ cup) crunchy peanut butter

2 teaspoons natural vanilla extract

30 g (1 oz/¼ cup) plain (all-purpose) flour

30 g (1 oz/⅓ cup) ground almonds

½ teaspoon mixed (pumpkin pie) spice

300 g (10½ oz/3 cups) quick-cooking oats

2 teaspoons finely grated orange zest

185 g (6½ oz/1 cup) soft brown sugar

45 g (1½ oz/½ cup) desiccated coconut

50 g (1¾ oz/⅓ cup) sesame seeds, toasted

90 g (3¼ oz/½ cup) pepitas or shelled sunflower seeds

80 g (2¾ oz/½ cup) raisins, chopped

45 g (1½ oz/¼ cup) mixed peel

1 Preheat the oven to 170°C (325°F/Gas 3). Lightly grease a 20 x 30 cm (8 x 12 inch) shallow tin and line with baking paper, leaving it hanging over the two long sides.

2 Place the butter and golden syrup in a small saucepan over low heat, stirring occasionally until melted. Remove from the heat and stir in the peanut butter and vanilla until well combined.

3 Mix together the remaining ingredients, stirring well. Make a well in the centre and add the butter and syrup mixture. Mix with a large metal spoon until combined. Press evenly into the tin and bake for 25 minutes, or until golden and firm. Cool in the tin, then cut into squares.

GLACE FRUIT SLICE

MAKES 24

480 g (1 lb 1 oz/2 cups) roughly chopped glacé fruit

2 tablespoons rum

100 g (3¼ oz/3½ oz) unsalted butter, softened

90 g (⅓ cup) caster (superfine) sugar

2 eggs

2 teaspoons natural vanilla extract

125 g (4½ oz/1 cup) mixed toasted nuts, roughly chopped

30 g (1 oz/¼ cup) plain (all-purpose) flour, sifted

30 g (1 oz/¼ cup) self-raising flour, sifted

25 g (1 oz/¼ cup) milk powder

80 g (2¾ oz/⅔ cup) icing (confectioners') sugar

1 teaspoon rum, extra

1 **Preheat the oven** to 190°C (375°F/Gas 5). Lightly grease an 18 x 27 cm (7 x 10½ inch) shallow baking tin and line with baking paper, leaving it hanging over on the two long sides.

2 **Combine the glacé** fruit and rum in a bowl. Beat the butter and sugar with electric beaters until light and fluffy. Add the eggs one at a time, beating well after each addition. Beat in the vanilla, then stir in the fruit mixture, nuts, flours and milk powder.

3 **Spread evenly** into the tin. Bake for 15 minutes. Reduce the oven to 180°C (350°F/Gas 4) and bake for 10 minutes, or until golden brown. Cool in the tin until just warm.

4 **Combine the icing sugar,** extra rum and 1 teaspoon water until smooth and spreadable but not runny. If the icing is too thick, add a little more rum or water. Spread over the slice and cool completely. Cut into three lengthways strips, then cut each strip into eight pieces.

CIDER CRUMBLE SLICE

MAKES 24

60 g (2¼ oz) unsalted butter

1½ tablespoons golden syrup

150 ml (5 fl oz/⅔ cup) alcoholic apple cider

250 g (9 oz/2 cups) self-raising flour

⅛ teaspoon ground ginger

50 g (1¾ oz/¼ cup) soft brown sugar

70 g (⅓ cup) stoned dates, chopped

150 g (5½ oz/1½ cups) walnuts, chopped

1 egg

1 large granny smith apple

2½ tablespoons caster (superfine) sugar

60 g (2¼ oz/½ cup) plain (all-purpose) flour

1   Preheat the oven to 170°C (325°F/Gas 3). Lightly grease a 20 x 30 cm (8 x 12 inch) baking tin and line with baking paper, leaving it hanging over on the long sides.

2   Melt 20 g (½ oz) of the butter and the golden syrup in a saucepan. Remove from heat and stir in the cider. Sift the flour and ginger into a bowl. Stir in the brown sugar, dates and half the nuts. Beat in the golden syrup mixture and egg until smooth. Spoon into the tin.

3   Peel, core and thinly slice the apple, then cut into 1.5 cm (½ in) pieces. Melt the remaining butter in a small saucepan, add the caster sugar, flour, apple and remaining nuts and stir well. Spread over the cake mixture. Bake for 30 minutes, or until golden and a skewer comes out clean. Cool in the tin, remove and cut into squares.

RUM AND RAISIN SLICE

MAKES 20

60 g (2¼ oz/½ cup) raisins

80 ml (2⅓ fl oz/⅓ cup) dark rum

200 g (7 oz) dark chocolate

60 g (2¼ oz) unsalted butter

125 g (4½ oz/½ cup) caster (superfine) sugar

250 ml (9 fl oz) 1 cup) thick (double/heavy) cream

125 g (4½ oz/1 cup) plain (all-purpose) flour

3 eggs, lightly beaten

cocoa powder, to dust

1   Preheat the oven to 180°C (350°F/Gas 4). Lightly grease an 18 x 28 cm (7 x 11¼ inch) shallow baking tin and line with baking paper, leaving it hanging over on two opposite sides.

2   Combine the raisins and rum. Chop the chocolate and butter into small even-sized pieces and place in a heatproof bowl. Bring a saucepan of water to the boil and remove from the heat. Sit the bowl over the pan — ensure the bowl doesn't touch the water. Allow to stand, stirring occasionally until melted. Stir in the caster sugar and cream.

3   Sift the flour into a bowl. Add the raisins, chocolate mixture and eggs and mix well. Pour into the tin and smooth the surface. Bake for 25–30 minutes, or until just set. Cool completely, then refrigerate overnight. To serve, cut into small pieces and sprinkle generously with cocoa powder.

STICKY TOFFEE SLICE

MAKES 18

250 g (9 oz/1⅓ cups) stoned dates,
   roughly chopped

1 teaspoon bicarbonate of soda
   (baking soda)

220 g (8 oz) unsalted butter

185 g (6½ oz/1½ cups) self-raising flour

1 teaspoon natural vanilla extract

1 teaspoon baking powder

3 eggs

90 ml (3 fl oz/⅓ cup) milk

2 tablespoons soft brown sugar

90 g (3¼ oz/¾ cup) icing
   (confectioners') sugar

90 g (3¼ oz/¾ cup) chopped walnuts

1 **Preheat the oven** to 180°C (350°F/Gas 4). Lightly grease a 20 x 30 cm (8 x 12 inch) baking tin and line with baking paper, hanging over the two long sides.

2 **Place the dates** in a saucepan with 200 ml water, bring to the boil, then reduce the heat and simmer gently for 10 minutes — make sure the water doesn't evaporate completely. Add the bicarbonate of soda and leave to cool.

3 **Place 185 g** (6 oz) of the butter, the flour, vanilla extract, baking powder, eggs and 75 ml (2¼ fl oz) of the milk in a food processor and mix in short bursts for about 1 minute, or until well blended. Add dates and pulse to blend. Do not overprocess the mixture.

4 **Place the mixture** in the tin and bake for 20 minutes, or until a skewer inserted in the centre comes out clean. Set aside to cool.

5 **Place the remaining butter** and milk and the brown sugar in a pan and heat gently to dissolve the sugar. Add the icing sugar and mix well. Spread over the cooled slice and sprinkle with the walnuts.

GINGER PANFORTE SLICE

MAKES 20

40 g (1½ oz/⅓ cup) plain (all-purpose) flour

1 tablespoon cocoa powder

1 teaspoon ground ginger

½ teaspoon ground cardamom

1 teaspoon ground cinnamon

125 g (4½ oz/¾ cup) dried figs, chopped

50 g (1¾ oz/¼ cup) glacé ginger, chopped

50 g (1¾ oz/¼ cup) glacé pineapple, chopped

50 g (1¾ oz/¼ cup) glacé apricots, chopped

50 g (1¾ oz/¼ cup) chopped mixed peel (mixed candied cirtus peel)

175 g (6 oz/1 cup) blanched almonds, toasted

90 g (3¼ oz/⅓ cup) caster (superfine) sugar

90 g (3¼ oz/¼ cup) honey

1 Preheat the oven to 160°C (315°F/Gas 2–3). Lightly grease a 7 x 25 cm (2¾ x 10 inch) shallow baking tin and line with baking paper, leaving it hanging over at the two short ends.

2 Sift the flour, cocoa, ginger and spices into a large bowl. Add the fruit and almonds.

3 Heat the caster sugar, honey and 2 teaspoons water in a small saucepan over low heat, stirring until melted and it just comes to the boil. Pour onto the dry ingredients and mix well. Press the mixture into the tin and bake for 35–40 minutes, or until just firm. Cool in the tin, then chill until firm. Cut into thin slices.

LEMON RICOTTA SLICE

MAKES 15

220 g (7¾ oz/1¾ cups) plain (all-purpose) flour

1 teaspoon baking powder

180 g (6½ oz) unsalted butter, melted

210 g (7½ oz/1 cup) caster (superfine) sugar

4 eggs

350 g (12 oz/1⅓ cups) ricotta cheese

200 ml (7 fl oz/¾ cup) cream

2 tablespoons lemon zest

185 ml (6 fl oz/¾ cup) lemon juice

icing (confectioners') sugar, to dust

1 **Preheat the oven** to 180°C (350°F/Gas 4). Lightly grease a 20 x 30 cm (8 x 12 inch) baking tin and line with baking paper, leaving it hanging over the two long sides.

2 **Put the flour,** baking powder, butter and half of the caster sugar in a food processor and process in short bursts until the mixture comes together in a ball. Add 1 egg and process until combined.

3 **Press the mixture** into the tin. Bake for 15 minutes. Remove from the oven. Reduce the oven to 150°C (300°F/Gas 2).

4 **Place the ricotta,** cream, lemon zest and juice, the remaining sugar and remaining eggs in the cleaned food processor and combine the ingredients for 1–2 seconds. Pour onto the pastry base and bake for 25–30 minutes — the slice will still have a slight wobble at this stage. Cool slightly, then refrigerate for 2 hours to firm. Cut into pieces. Dust with icing sugar and serve.

JAFFA FUDGE SLICE

MAKES 32

200 g (6½ oz) plain sweet
    chocolate biscuits (cookies)

125 g (4½ oz/1 cup) chopped walnuts

125 g (4½ oz) dark chocolate, chopped

60 g (2¼ oz/½ cup) icing
    (confectioners') sugar

125 g (4½ oz) butter

1 tablespoon grated orange rind

125 g (4½ oz) dark chocolate, extra,
    melted

1 Lightly grease an 18 x 28 cm (7 x 11 inch) shallow tin and line with baking paper or foil, overhanging two opposite sides.

2 Place the biscuits and walnuts in a food processor and process until the mixture resembles coarse breadcrumbs. Transfer to a large mixing bowl and make a well in the centre.

3 Put the chopped chocolate, sifted icing sugar and butter in a small saucepan and stir over low heat until melted and smooth. Remove from the heat, stir in the orange rind, then pour into the biscuit mixture and stir until well combined.

4 Press the mixture firmly into the prepared tin. Chill for 10 minutes. Spread the melted chocolate over and chill for 30 minutes to set.

Note: Slices can be kept in an airtight container for up to a week.

ORANGE, PISTACHIO AND SEMOLINA SLICE

MAKES 18

100 g (3½ oz/⅔ cup) shelled pistachio nuts

200 g (7 oz) unsalted butter, chopped

160 g (5¾ oz/⅔ cup) caster (superfine) sugar

1 teaspoon natural vanilla extract

1 tablespoon finely grated orange zest

2 eggs

60 g (2¼ oz/½ cup) self-raising flour, sifted

125 ml (4 fl oz/½ cup) orange juice

185 g (6½ oz/1½ cups) fine semolina

250 g (9 oz/1 cup) caster (superfine) sugar, extra

125 ml (4 fl oz/½ cup) orange juice, extra

icing (confectioners') sugar, to dust

1 **Preheat the oven** to 180°C (350°F/Gas 4). Lightly grease a 20 x 30 cm (8 x 12 inch) shallow baking tin and line with baking paper, leaving it hanging over on the two long sides.

2 **Bake the pistachios** for 8–10 minutes, or until they are lightly toasted. Cool, then chop.

3 **Beat the butter** and sugar with electric beaters until light and fluffy. Add the vanilla, orange zest and eggs, and beat until combined.

4 **Add the flour,** orange juice, semolina and pistachio nuts, and fold in with a spatula until just combined — do not overmix. Spread into the tin. Bake for 30 minutes, or until golden brown and firm when lightly touched. Cool for 10 minutes in the tin, then on a wire rack placed on a tray.

5 **Mix the extra sugar** and orange juice in a small saucepan. Bring to the boil over medium heat, then simmer for 1 minute. Spoon over the slice. Cool and cut into squares or diamonds. Dust with icing sugar.

CHOCOLATE AND GLACE CHERRY SLICE

MAKES 28

125 g (4½ oz/1 cup) plain (all-purpose) flour

40 g (1½ oz/⅓ cup) cocoa powder

90 g (3¼ oz/⅓ cup) caster (superfine) sugar

125 g unsalted butter, melted

1 teaspoon natural vanilla extract

420 g (15 oz/2 cups) glacé cherries, finely chopped

60 g (2¼ oz/½ cup) icing (confectioners') sugar

135 g (4¾ oz/1½ cups) desiccated coconut

160 g (5¾ oz/½ cup) condensed milk

60 g (2¼ oz) unsalted butter, melted

50 g (1¾ oz) Copha (white vegetable shortening), melted

150 g (5½ oz) dark cooking chocolate

25 g (1 oz) unsalted butter, extra

1 Preheat the oven to 180°C (350°F/Gas 4). Lightly grease an 18 x 27 cm (7 x 10¾ inch) shallow baking tin and line with baking paper, leaving the paper hanging over the two long sides.

2 Sift the flour, cocoa and sugar into a bowl, add the butter and vanilla, and mix to form a dough. Gather together and turn onto a well-floured surface. Press together for 1 minute, then press into the base of the tin. Chill for 20 minutes. Cover with baking paper and baking beads or uncooked rice and bake for 10–15 minutes. Remove the paper and beads and bake for 5 minutes. Cool.

3 Combine the cherries, icing sugar and coconut. Stir in the condensed milk, butter and Copha, then spread over the base. Chill for 30 minutes.

4 Chop the chocolate and extra butter into small even-sized pieces and place in a heatproof bowl. Bring a saucepan of water to the boil and remove from the heat. Sit the bowl over the pan, making sure the bowl doesn't touch the water. Allow to stand, stirring occasionally until melted. Pour over the cooled cherry mixture, then chill until set.

CHOCOLATE CHEESE SLICE

MAKES 24

1.25 kg (2 lb 12 oz) cream cheese, at room temperature

120 g (4¼ oz/½ cup) ricotta cheese

3 teaspoons natural vanilla extract

310 g (11 oz/1¼ cups) caster (superfine) sugar

6 eggs

100 g (3½ oz/²/₃ cup) dark chocolate, broken into pieces

1 tablespoon milk

2 teaspoons powdered drinking chocolate

75 g (2½ oz/²/₃ cup) ground hazelnuts

3 teaspoons grated orange zest

50 g (1¾ oz) crushed amaretti biscuits

icing (confectioners') sugar, to dust

1 **Preheat the oven** to 170°C (325°F/Gas 3). Lightly grease a 20 x 30 cm (8 x 12 inch) shallow baking tin. Line with baking paper, extending over the two long sides.

2 **Blend the cream cheese,** ricotta, vanilla and sugar in a food processor until smooth. Add the eggs and process until smooth. Divide the mixture between two bowls.

3 **Bring a saucepan of water** to the boil and remove from the heat. Put the chocolate, milk and drinking chocolate in a heatproof bowl and place over the water. Make sure the bowl doesn't touch the water. Stir occasionally until melted. Cool. Add to one of the bowls of cream cheese. Mix well, then stir in the hazelnuts. Pour into the tin.

4 **Stir the orange zest** and biscuits into the other bowl of cream cheese. Mix well, then gently spoon over the chocolate mix, covering it completely.

5 **With a knife** and starting in one corner, cut the orange mix down through the chocolate, bringing the chocolate up in swirls through the orange.

6 **Bake for 1 hour,** or until set. Cool in the tin. Lift out and cut into squares. Dust with icing sugar to serve.

MUFFINS

DOUBLE CHOCOLATE CHIP MUFFINS

MAKES 12

310 g (11 oz/2½ cups) self-raising flour

60 g (2¼ oz/½ cup) cocoa powder

½ teaspoon bicarbonate of soda
  (baking soda)

165 g (5¾ oz/¾ cup) firmly packed soft
  brown sugar

175 g (6 oz/1 cup) milk choc bits

175 g (6 oz/1 cup) white choc bits or
  chopped white choc melts

315 ml 10¾ fl oz/1¼ cups) milk

2 eggs

100 g (3½ oz) unsalted butter, melted
  and cooled

1 **Preheat the oven** to 200°C (400°F/Gas 6). Lightly grease a 12-hole standard muffin tin. Sift flour, cocoa and bicarbonate of soda into a large bowl. Stir in the sugar and 130 g (4½ oz/ ¾ cup) each of the choc bits. Make a well in the centre.

2 **Whisk together the milk,** eggs and butter in a bowl and pour into the well. Fold gently — the batter should be lumpy.

3 **Divide the batter** among the muffin holes. Sprinkle with the remaining choc bits and bake for 20–25 minutes, or until the muffins come away from the side of the tin. Cool, then transfer to a wire rack.

BLUEBERRY MUFFINS

MAKES 12

375 g (13 oz/3 cups) plain (all-purpose) flour

1 tablespoon baking powder

165 g (5¾ oz/¾ cup) firmly packed soft brown sugar

125 g (4½ oz) unsalted butter, melted

2 eggs, lightly beaten

250 ml (9 fl oz/1 cup) milk

185 g (6½ oz/1⅓ cup) fresh or thawed, frozen blueberries

1 Preheat the oven to 210°C (415°F/Gas 6–7). Lightly grease a 12-hole standard muffin tins. Sift the flour and baking powder into a large mixing bowl. Stir in the sugar and make a well in the centre of the dry ingredients.

2 In a separate mixing bowl, add the melted butter, eggs and milk and stir to combine. Add all at once to the flour mixture and fold until just combined. (Do not overmix, the batter should look quite lumpy.)

3 Fold in the blueberries. Spoon the batter into the prepared tin. Bake for 20 minutes, or until golden brown. Turn out onto a wire rack to cool.

LEMON SYRUP MUFFINS

MAKES 12

310 g (11 oz/2½ cups) self-raising flour

310 g (11 oz/1¼ cups) caster (superfine) sugar

125 g (4½ oz/½ cup) plain yoghurt

80 ml (2½ fl oz/⅓ cup) milk

1 egg

250 ml (9 fl oz/1 cup) lemon juice

2 tablespoons finely grated lemon zest

110 g (3¾ oz) unsalted butter, melted and cooled

60 g (2¼ oz/¼ cup) ready-made lemon butter

1 **Preheat the oven** to 200°C (400°F/Gas 6). Lightly grease a 12-hole standard muffin tin. Sift the flour into a large bowl, add 185 g (6½ oz/¾ cup) sugar and combine. Make a well in the centre.

2 **Put the yoghurt,** milk, egg, half the lemon juice and 1 tablespoon of the lemon zest in a bowl, whisk together and pour into the well. Add the butter. Fold gently until just combined — the batter should be lumpy.

3 **Divide half the batter** among the muffin holes. Put 1 teaspoon of lemon butter in the centre of each, then cover with the remaining batter. Bake for 20 minutes, or until they come away from the side of the tin. Cool for 5 minutes.

4 **Meanwhile,** to make the syrup, place the remaining sugar, juice and rind in a small saucepan. Stir over medium heat until the sugar dissolves, then simmer for 5 minutes. Keep hot.

5 **Place the muffins** on a wire rack with a tray underneath and drizzle with syrup. Serve warm.

ZUCCHINI AND CARROT MUFFINS

MAKES 12

250 g (9 oz/2 cups) self-raising flour

1 teaspoon ground cinnamon

½ teaspoon ground nutmeg

2 carrots, peeled and grated

2 zucchini (courgettes), grated

60 g (2¼ oz/½ cup) chopped pecans

2 eggs

250 ml (9 fl oz/1 cup) milk

90 g (3¼ oz) unsalted butter, melted

1 **Preheat the oven** to 210°C (415°F/Gas 6–7). Lightly grease a 12-hole standard muffin tin.

2 **Sift the flour,** cinnamon, nutmeg and a pinch of sea salt into a large bowl. Add the carrot, zucchini and pecans and stir well.

3 **Put the eggs,** milk and melted butter in a separate bowl and whisk together well.

4 **Make a well** in the centre of the flour mixture, then add the egg mixture all at once. Mix quickly using a fork until all the ingredients are just moistened. Do not overmix — the batter should still be lumpy.

5 **Spoon the batter** into the muffin holes and bake for 15–20 minutes, or until golden. Remove from the oven and loosen the muffins with a flat-bladed knife or spatula. Leave to cool in the tin for 2 minutes before turning out onto a wire rack to cool slightly. Serve warm.

PLAIN MUFFINS

MAKES 12

310 g (11 oz/2½ cups) self-raising flour

60 g (2¼ oz/¼ cup) caster (superfine) sugar

2 teaspoons baking powder

2 eggs, lightly beaten

310 ml (10¾ fl oz/1¼ cups) milk

160 g (5½ oz) unsalted butter, melted

1 **Preheat the oven** to 210°C (415°F/Gas 6–7). Lightly grease a 12-hole standard muffin tin.

2 **Sift the flour,** sugar and baking powder into a large mixing bowl. Make a well in the centre.

3 **Place the egg,** milk and butter in a separate mixing bowl. Combine and add all at once to the flour mixture. Stir gently with a fork or rubber spatula until the mixture is just moistened. Do not overmix as the batter should look quite lumpy.

4 **Spoon the mixture** evenly into the prepared muffin holes until two-thirds full. Bake for 20–25 minutes, or until golden brown. Loosen the muffins with a flat-bladed knife and transfer to a wire rack to cool.

EBONY AND IVORY MUFFINS

MAKES 12

250 g (9 oz/2cups) plain
(all-purpose) flour

1 tablespoon baking powder

90 g (3¼ oz/⅓ cup) caster
(superfine) sugar

250 g (9 oz/1 cup) vanilla yoghurt

2 eggs

125 g (4½ oz) unsalted butter, melted
and cooled

180 g (6 oz) dark cooking chocolate,
melted

60 g (2¼ oz/½ cup) chopped walnuts

80 g (2¼ oz/½ cup) chopped blanched
almonds

2 teaspoons finely grated orange zest

1 **Preheat the oven** to 200°C (400°F/Gas 6). Lightly grease a 12-hole standard muffin tin. Sift the flour and baking powder into a large bowl and add the sugar and a pinch of salt. Stir, then make a well in the centre. Combine the yoghurt, eggs and butter, then pour into the well.

2 **Fold gently** until just combined — the batter should be lumpy. Transfer half the batter to another bowl.

3 **Fold the chocolate** and walnuts into one bowl of batter and the almonds and orange zest into the other.

4 **Spoon chocolate batter** into one side of each muffin hole and almond batter into the other side. Bake for 20 minutes, or until the muffins come away from the side of the tin. Cool for 5 minutes, then transfer to a wire rack.

CHOCOLATE CHIP MUFFINS

MAKES 12

310 g (11 oz/2½ cups) self-raising flour

265 g (9½ oz/1½ cups) chocolate chips

95 g (3½ oz/½ cup) soft brown sugar

375 ml (13 fl oz/1½ cups) milk

2 eggs, lightly beaten

1 teaspoon natural vanilla extract

150 g (5½ oz) unsalted butter,
    melted and cooled

1   Preheat the oven to 200°C (400°F/Gas 6). Lightly grease a 12-hole standard muffin tin, or line a muffin tin with paper cases. Sift the flour into a bowl. Add the chocolate chips and sugar to the bowl and stir through the flour. Make a well in the centre.

2   Combine the milk, egg and vanilla. Pour the liquid into the well in the flour and add the cooled butter. Fold the mixture gently with a metal spoon until just combined. Do not overmix — the batter will still be slightly lumpy. Divide evenly among the holes, filling each one to about three-quarters full.

3   Bake the muffins for 20–25 minutes, or until they are golden and a skewer inserted in the centre of a muffin comes out clean. Leave the muffins in the tin for 2 minutes to cool. Gently loosen each one with a flat-bladed knife before turning out onto a wire rack. Serve warm or at room temperature.

ORANGE-FROSTED CARROT MUFFINS

MAKES 12

250 g (9 oz/2 cups) self-raising flour

¾ teaspoon mixed (pumpkin pie) spice

1 teaspoon bicarbonate of soda

1 tablespoon ground almonds

165 g (5¾ oz/¾cup) raw (demerara) sugar

1 tablespoon golden syrup

75 g (2½ oz) unsalted butter

60 ml (2 fl oz/¼ cup) milk

3 eggs, lightly beaten

1¼ teaspoons natural vanilla extract

150 ml (5 fl oz) oil

410 g (14½ oz/2⅔ cups) firmly packed grated carrot

250 g (9 oz/2 cups) roughly chopped pecans

ICING (FROSTING)

180 g (6 oz) cream cheese

25 g (1 oz) unsalted butter, softened

¾ teaspoon orange zest

1½ tablespoons orange juice

60 g (2¼ oz/½ cup) icing (confectioners') sugar

1 **Preheat the oven** to 180°C (350°F/Gas 4). Grease 12 large muffin holes. Sift the flour, spice and bicarbonate of soda into a large bowl and add the almonds, sugar and a pinch of salt. Make a well in the centre.

2 **Melt the golden syrup** and butter in a small saucepan over low heat. Remove from the heat, cool, then stir in the milk, egg, vanilla and oil. Pour into the well. Fold until just combined — the batter should be lumpy. Stir in the carrot and pecans.

3 **Divide among** the muffin holes. Bake for 30–35 minutes, or until the muffins come away from the side of the tin. Cool for 5 minutes, then transfer to a wire rack.

4 **Put the cream cheese,** butter and zest in a bowl and beat until fluffy. Beat in the juice and icing sugar. Chill for 30 minutes, then spread on the muffins.

CHOCOLATE MUFFINS WITH A CREAM CHEESE CENTRE

MAKES 12

280 g (10 oz/2¼ cups) plain (all-purpose) flour

40 g (1½ oz/⅓ cup) cocoa powder

1 teaspoon bicarbonate of soda (baking soda)

160 g (5 oz/⅔ cup) caster (superfine) sugar

185 ml (6 fl oz/¾ cup) milk

1 teaspoon natural vanilla extract

185 ml (6 fl oz/¾ cup) oil

cocoa powder, to dust

icing (confectioners') sugar, to dust

FILLING

100 g (3½ oz/⅓ cup) cream cheese, softened

2 tablespoons caster (superfine) sugar

½ teaspoon natural vanilla extract

90 g (3¼ oz/⅔ cup) white chocolate melts, melted

1 **Preheat the oven** to 180°C (350°F/Gas 4). Lightly grease a 12-hole standard muffin tin. Blend the cream cheese, sugar and vanilla in a bowl using electric beaters, then stir in the melted chocolate.

2 **Sift the flour,** cocoa and bicarbonate of soda into a large bowl and add the sugar. Make a well in the centre.

3 **Whisk the milk,** vanilla and oil together in a bowl and pour into the well. Fold gently until just combined — the batter should be lumpy.

4 **Fill each muffin hole** one-third full with the batter. Place a tablespoon of the filling into each muffin hole and top with the remaining batter. Bake for 20 minutes, or until the muffins come away from the side of the tin. Cool briefly, then transfer to a wire rack. Dust with cocoa and icing sugar. Serve warm.

FIG AND OAT BRAN MUFFINS

MAKES 12

125 g (4½ oz/1 cup) self-raising flour

75 g (2½ oz/½ cup) wholemeal self-raising flour

½ teaspoon baking powder

150 g (5½ oz/1 cup) oat bran

55 g (2 oz/¼ cup) firmly packed soft brown sugar

250 ml (9 fl oz/1 cup) milk

2 eggs

90 g (3¼ oz/¼ cup) golden syrup (dark corn syrup)

60 g (2¼ oz) unsalted butter, melted and cooled

185 g (6½ oz/1 cup) soft dried figs, chopped

3 dried figs, cut into strips, extra

1 **Preheat the oven** to 200°C (400°F/Gas 6). Lightly grease a 12-hole standard muffin tin. Sift flours and baking powder into a bowl, add oat bran and sugar. Make a well in the centre.

2 **Place the milk** and eggs in a bowl, whisk together and pour into the well. Add the combined golden syrup and butter and fold gently until just combined — the batter should be lumpy. Fold in the chopped figs.

3 **Divide the mixture** among the muffin holes and top with the extra strips of fig. Bake for 20–25 minutes, or until the muffins come away from the side of the tin. Cool in the tin for 5 minutes, then transfer to a wire rack.

STICKY GINGERBREAD MUFFINS

MAKES 12

250 g (9 oz/2 cups) self-raising flour

90 g (3¼ oz/¾ cup) plain (all-purpose) flour

½ teaspoon bicarbonate of soda (baking soda)

3 teaspoons ground ginger

1 teaspoon ground cinnamon

1 teaspoon mixed (pumpkin pie) spice

230 g (8 oz/1 cup) firmly packed soft brown sugar

55 g (2 oz/¼ cup) chopped glacé ginger

235 g (8½ oz/⅔ cup) golden syrup

100g (3½ oz) unsalted butter, chopped

250 ml (9 fl oz/1 cup) buttermilk

1 egg, lightly beaten

GINGER ICING (FROSTING)

60 g (2¼ oz) unsalted butter, softened

1½ tablespoons golden syrup

1 cup (125 g) icing (confectioners') sugar

½ teaspoon ground ginger

50 g (1¾ oz/⅓ cup) dark chocolate, chopped into even-sized pieces

1 **Preheat the oven** to 200°C (400°F/Gas 6). Lightly grease a 12-hole standard muffin tin. Sift the self-raising and plain flours, bicarbonate of soda, ginger, cinnamon and mixed spice into a large bowl and stir in the brown sugar and glacé ginger. Make a well in the centre.

2 **Place the golden syrup** and butter in a small saucepan and stir over medium heat until melted and well mixed. Remove from the heat and cool.

3 **Combine the golden syrup** mixture, buttermilk and egg in a large bowl. Pour into the well in the dry ingredients. Fold gently until just combined — the batter should be lumpy.

4 **Divide the mixture** evenly among the muffin holes. Bake for 20–25 minutes, or until the muffins come away from the side of the tin. Cool for 5 minutes in the tin, then transfer to a wire rack to cool completely.

5 **To make the ginger frosting,** beat the butter, golden syrup, icing sugar and ground ginger together with electric beaters in a bowl until light and fluffy. Spread evenly over the top of the cooled muffins.

6 **Place the chocolate pieces** in a heatproof bowl. Bring a saucepan of water to the boil, then remove from the heat. Sit the bowl over the saucepan, making sure the base of the bowl does not sit in the water. Stir occasionally until the chocolate has melted. Cool for 5 minutes.

7 **Spoon the melted chocolate** into the corner of a plastic sandwich bag. Snip off the tip of the filled corner to create a nozzle. Pipe the chocolate over the icing in thin criss-crossing lines. Apply even pressure and work at a steady speed to stop the chocolate from clumping. Leave the chocolate to set before serving the muffins.

MUESLI MUFFINS

MAKES 6

95 g (3¼ oz/½ cup) dried apricots, chopped

125 ml (4 fl oz/½ cup) orange juice

2 teaspoons finely grated orange zest

150 g (5½ oz/1 cup) wholemeal self-raising flour

60 g (2¼ oz/½ cup) self-raising flour

½ teaspoon baking powder

45 g (1½ oz/¼ cup) soft brown sugar

75 g (2½ oz/¾ cup) toasted muesli

250 ml (9 fl oz/1 cup) milk

60 g (2¼ oz) unsalted butter, melted

TOPPING

1 tablespoon plain (all-purpose) flour

½ teaspoon ground cinnamon

45 g (1½ oz/¼ cup) soft brown sugar

35 g (1¼ oz/⅓ cup) toasted muesli

20 g (¾ oz) butter, melted

1 **Preheat the oven** to 210°C (415°F/Gas 6–7). Lightly grease a 6-hole large muffin tin. Combine the apricots, orange juice and zest in a bowl. Set mixture aside for 20 minutes.

2 **Sift the flours** and baking powder into a mixing bowl. Add the sugar and muesli and stir through.

3 **Combine the milk,** melted butter and undrained apricot mixture. Add to dry ingredients. Mix quickly with a fork until all ingredients are just moistened.

4 **Spoon the mixture** evenly into the prepared tin. Sprinkle with topping. Bake the muffins for 20–25 minutes, or until golden brown. Loosen muffins with a flat-bladed knife and turn out onto a wire rack to cool completely.

5 **To make the topping,** place the flour, cinnamon, sugar, muesli and butter in a bowl. Stir to combine.

Note: The muffins can be frozen for up to 3 months. Reheat in a 180°C (350°F/ Gas 4) oven for 10 minutes.

WHITE CHOCOLATE MANGO MUFFINS

MAKES 12

310 g (11 oz/2½ cups) self-raising flour

95 g (3¼ oz/½ cup) soft brown sugar

130 g (4½ oz/¾ cup) white chocolate chips

315 g (11 oz/1 cup) chopped fresh mango flesh (2 medium) or 440 g (15½ oz) tin mango pieces, well drained

125 ml (4 fl oz/½ cup) milk

60 ml (2 fl oz/¼ cup) cream

90 g (3¼ oz) unsalted butter, melted

1 egg, lightly beaten

1 Preheat the oven to 180°C (350°F/Gas 4). Lightly grease a 12-hole standard muffin tin. Sift the flour into a large mixing bowl. Stir in sugar and choc chips and mix well. Gently fold in the chopped mango. Make a well in the centre of the mixture.

2 Add the combined milk, cream, butter and egg all at once. Mix with a fork or rubber spatula until just combined. Do not overmix, the batter should look quite lumpy. Spoon the mixture into the prepared tin.

3 Bake for 20 minutes, or until the muffins come away from the side of the tin. Loosen the muffins with a flat-bladed knife and turn out onto a wire rack to cool completely.

Note: Serve these muffins warm with whipped cream. They also make a delicious dessert, served warm and topped with large shavings of white chocolate or served split with stewed apples or peaches.

APPLE AND BERRY CRUMBLE MUFFINS

MAKES 12

155 g (5½ oz/1¼ cups) self-raising flour

150 g (5½ oz/1 cup) wholemeal self-raising flour

¼ teaspoon ground cinnamon

pinch ground cloves

115 g (4 oz/½ cup) firmly packed soft brown sugar

185 ml (6 fl oz/¾ cup) milk

2 eggs

125 g (4½ oz) unsalted butter, melted and cooled

2 granny smith apples, peeled, cored, grated

155 g (5½ oz/1 cup) blueberries

CRUMBLE

5 tablespoons plain (all-purpose) flour

55g (2 oz/¼ cup) raw (demerara) sugar

35 g (1¼ oz/⅓ cup) rolled oats

40 g (1½ oz) unsalted butter, chopped

1 Preheat the oven to 190°C (375°F/Gas 5). Line a 12-hole standard muffin tin with paper cases. Sift the flours, cinnamon and cloves into a large bowl and stir in the sugar. Make a well in the centre.

2 Put the milk, eggs and butter in a bowl, whisk and pour into the well. Fold gently until just combined — the batter should be lumpy. Fold in the fruit. Divide the mixture among the muffin holes.

3 To make the crumble, put the flour, sugar and oats in a bowl. Rub the butter in with your fingertips until most of the lumps are gone. Sprinkle 2 teaspoons of the crumble over each muffin. Bake for 25 minutes, or until golden. Cool for 5 minutes, then transfer to a wire rack.

BANANA MUFFINS

MAKES 12

250 g (9 oz/2 cups) self-raising flour

75 g (2½ oz/1 cup) oat bran

185 g (6½ oz/¾ cup) caster (superfine) sugar

60 g (2¼ oz) unsalted butter, melted

185 ml (6 fl oz/¾ cup) milk

2 eggs, lightly beaten

240 g (8½ oz/1 cup) mashed, ripe banana (2 medium bananas)

1 **Preheat the oven** to 210°C (415°F/Gas 6–7). Lightly grease a 12-hole standard muffin tin. Sift the flour into a large bowl and add the oat bran and the sugar. Make a well in the centre of the dry ingredients.

2 **Combine the butter,** milk, eggs and banana in a separate mixing bowl and add to the flour mixture all at once. Using a wooden spoon, stir until just mixed. Do not overmix — the batter should remain lumpy.

3 **Spoon mixture** into the prepared tin. Bake for 15 minutes, or until puffed and brown. Leave in tin for 5 minutes and then turn out onto a wire rack to cool completely.

Note: For an extra treat, beat 100 g (3½ oz) cream cheese, 2 tablespoons icing sugar and 2 teaspoons lemon juice with electric beaters until light and creamy. Spread over muffins and top with dried banana slices.

PEAR AND MUESLI MUFFINS

MAKES 12

225 g (8 oz/1½ cups) toasted muesli

1 tablespoon plain (all-purpose) flour

115 g (4 oz/½ cup) caster (superfine) sugar

90 g (3¼ oz) unsalted butter, melted

100 g (3¾ oz/½ cup) chopped, dried pears

125 ml (4 fl oz/½ cup) orange juice

1 tablespoon finely grated lemon zest

250 g (9 oz/2 cups) self-raising flour

½ teaspoon baking powder

250 ml (9 fl oz/1 cup) buttermilk

60 ml (2 fl oz/¼ cup) milk

90 g (3¼ oz/¼ cup) honey

1 **To make the topping,** place 75 g (2½ oz/½ cup) of the muesli, the plain flour and half the sugar in a small bowl and mix in 2 tablespoons of the butter until combined.

2 **Preheat the oven** to 200°C (400°F/Gas 6). Lightly grease a 12-hole standard muffin tin. Put the pears in a large bowl and add the orange juice and zest. Leave for 10 minutes.

3 **Sift the self-raising flour** and baking powder into the bowl with the pears and add the remaining muesli and sugar. Make a well in the centre.

4 **Whisk the buttermilk** and milk together in a bowl and pour into the well in the pear mixture. Combine the honey and remaining butter and add to the well. Fold until just combined — the batter should be lumpy.

5 **Divide the batter** among the muffin holes, then sprinkle on the topping. Bake for about 30 minutes, or until the muffins come away from the side of the tin. Cool briefly, then transfer to a wire rack. Serve warm with butter.

OATMEAL AND RASPBERRY MUFFINS

MAKES 12

125 g (4½ oz/1 cup) medium oatmeal

375 ml (13 fl oz/1½ cups) milk

250 g (9 oz/2 cups) plain
   (all-purpose) flour

1 tablespoon baking powder

115 g (4 oz/½ cup) soft brown sugar

1 egg, lightly beaten

90 g (3¼ oz/¼ cup) honey

60 g (2¼ oz) unsalted butter, melted

150 g (5½ oz/1¼ cups) raspberries

1 **Preheat the oven** to 190°C (375°F/Gas 5). Grease a 12-hole standard muffin tin, or line the holes with paper cases.

2 **Put the oatmeal** in a bowl, stir in the milk and set aside| for 5 minutes. Sift the flour and baking powder into a large bowl, then stir in the sugar. Make a well in the centre.

3 **Combine egg**, honey and butter in a bowl and stir to mix well. Pour egg mixture and oatmeal mixture into the well, then stir quickly until just combined. Do not overmix — the batter should be slightly lumpy. Gently fold in the raspberries.

4 **Divide the mixture** evenly between the muffin holes. Bake for 20–25 minutes, or until muffins are golden and a skewer inserted in the centre of a muffin comes out clean. Cool for 5 minutes before transferring to a wire rack. Serve warm.

LEMON MERINGUE MUFFINS

MAKES 12

215 g (7½ oz/1¾ cups) self-raising flour

185 g (6½ oz/¾ cup) caster (superfine) sugar

1 egg

1 egg yolk

170 ml (5½ fl oz/2/3 cup) milk

½ teaspoon natural vanilla extract

90 g (3¼ oz) unsalted butter, melted and cooled

200 g (7 oz/2/3 cup) ready-made lemon butter

2 egg whites

1 teaspoon caster (superfine) sugar, extra

1 Preheat the oven to 200°C (400°F/Gas 6). Lightly grease a 12-hole regular muffin tin. Sift flour into a large bowl and stir in 60 g (2¼ oz/ ¼ cup) of the sugar. Make a well in the centre.

2 Place the egg and egg yolk in a bowl and add a pinch of salt. Beat the egg mixture, then stir in the milk, vanilla and butter. Pour egg mixture into the well in the dry ingredients. Fold gently until just combined — the batter should be lumpy.

3 Divide the muffin mixture evenly among the muffin holes. Bake for 15 minutes — the muffins will only rise a little way up the muffin holes. (Leave the oven on at the same temperature.)

4 Cool the muffins in the tin for 10 minutes, then loosen with a knife but leave in the tin. Hollow out the centre of each muffin with a melon baller, taking care not to pierce the base.

5 Stir the lemon butter well, then spoon it into a piping bag fitted with a 1.25 cm (½ inch) plain nozzle.

6 Carefully pipe the lemon butter into the hollowed-out centre of each muffin.

7 Whisk the egg whites in a clean dry bowl until stiff peaks form. Add a quarter of the remaining sugar at a time, beating well after each addition until stiff and glossy peaks form.

8 Place a heaped tablespoon of the meringue mixture on top of each muffin and form peaks with the back of a spoon. Sprinkle a little extra caster sugar over the meringue.

9 Return muffins to the oven for 5 minutes, or until the meringue is lightly golden and crisp and the muffins come away slightly from the side of the tin. Cool muffins in tin for 10 minutes, then carefully transfer to a wire rack. Serve warm or at room temperature. These muffins are best eaten on the same day that they are made. The meringue will not stay crisp for longer.

HUMMINGBIRD MUFFINS

MAKES 12

215 g (7½ oz/1¾ cups) self-raising flour

275 g (9¾ oz/1½ cups) raw (demerara) sugar

2 teaspoons ground cinnamon

125 g (4½ oz/1 cup) chopped pecans

2 eggs

185 ml (6 fl oz/1 cup) oil

480 g (1 lb 1 oz/2 cups) mashed ripe banana

130 g (4½ oz/½ cup) drained crushed pineapple

6 pecans, halved (optional)

1   Preheat the oven to 180°C (350°F/Gas 4). Line a 12-hole standard muffin tin with muffin paper cases. Sift the flour into a bowl and stir in the sugar, cinnamon and pecans. Make a well in the centre.

2   Put the eggs and oil in a small bowl, whisk, then pour into the well. Add the banana and pineapple. Fold gently until just combined — the batter should be lumpy.

3   Divide among the muffin holes. Bake for 25–30 minutes, or until golden. Cool briefly, then transfer to a wire rack to cool completely. Top with pecans, if desired.

THREE CHEESE MUFFINS

MAKES 10

75 g (2½ oz) goat's cheese

3 tablespoons finely chopped fresh, flat-leaf (Italian) parsley

310 g (11 oz/2½ cups) self-raising flour

125 g (4½ oz/1 cup) grated cheddar cheese

65 g (2¼ oz/⅔ cup) finely grated parmesan cheese

315 ml (10¾ fl oz/1¼ cups) milk

1 egg

80 g (2¾ oz) butter, melted and cooled

1 **Preheat the oven** to 180°C (350°F/Gas 4). Grease a 10-hole standard muffin tin. Cut goat's cheese into 10 pieces, then roll them in the parsley until evenly coated.

2 **Sift the flour** and ½ teaspoon salt into a bowl and stir in the cheeses. Season, then make a well in the centre.

3 **Lightly whisk** together the milk, egg and butter in a bowl and pour into the well. Fold until combined — the batter should be lumpy.

4 **Divide the mixture** among the muffin holes. Top each muffin with a piece of herbed goat's cheese. Bake for about 20 minutes, or until golden. Cool for 5 minutes, then transfer to a wire rack.

STICKY DATE MUFFINS

MAKES 12

160 g (5½ oz/1 cup) stoned dates, chopped

1 teaspoon bicarbonate of soda (baking soda)

90g (3¼ oz) unsalted butter, softened

165 g (5¾ oz/¾ cup) firmly packed dark brown sugar

1 teaspoon natural vanilla extract

2 eggs

185 g (6½ oz/1½ cups) self-raising flour

60 g (2¼ oz/½ cup) plain (all-purpose) flour

170 ml (5½ fl oz/⅔ cup) pouring cream

155 g (5½ oz/⅔ cup) firmly packed dark brown sugar, extra

60 g (2¼ oz/½ cup) chopped walnuts

1 **Preheat the oven** to 200°C (400°F/Gas 6). Grease a 12-hole standard muffin tin. Place dates and 1 cup (250 ml/ 9 fl oz) water in a bowl, then add the bicarbonate of soda. Leave for 10 minutes. Sift the flours into a bowl.

2 **Put the butter,** sugar and vanilla in a bowl and beat with electric beaters. Add the eggs one at a time, beating well after each addition. Stir in the date mixture, then the sifted flours.

3 **Divide the mixture** among the muffin holes. Bake for 20–25 minutes, or until the muffins come away from the side of the tin. Cool slightly, then transfer to a wire rack that is sitting over a tray.

4 **Meanwhile,** put the cream and extra sugar in a small saucepan and stir over low heat until the sugar dissolves.

5 **Brush the muffins** with sauce, sprinkle with walnuts and serve.

JAM-FILLED MUFFINS

MAKES 12

340 g (11¾ oz/2¾ cups) self-raising flour

185 g (6½ oz/¾ cup) caster (superfine) sugar

250 ml (9 fl oz/1 cup) buttermilk

60 ml (2 fl oz/¼ cup) milk

2 eggs

1 teaspoon natural vanilla extract

100 g (3½ oz) unsalted butter, melted and cooled

200 g (7 oz) raspberries

105 g (3½ oz/⅓ cup) raspberry jam

100 g (3½ oz) unsalted butter, melted, extra

125 g (4½ oz/½ cup) caster (superfine) sugar, extra

1 **Preheat the oven** to 200°C (400°F/Gas 6). Grease 12 regular muffin holes. Sift the flour into a bowl and add the sugar. Make a well in the centre.

2 **Put the buttermilk,** milk, eggs, vanilla and butter in a bowl, whisk together and pour into the well. Fold mixture until just combined — the batter should be lumpy. Fold in the berries.

3 **Divide the mixture** among the muffin holes. Indent the centre of each muffin and fill with ½ teaspoon jam, then cover with batter.

4 **Bake the muffins** for 25–30 minutes, or until they come away from the side of the tin. Cool for 5 minutes, then transfer to a wire rack.

5 **Brush each muffin** all over with the extra melted butter, then roll in the combined extra sugar and cinnamon.

BACON AND EGG MUFFINS

MAKES 6

3 slices bacon, finely chopped

2 hard-boiled eggs, chopped

250 g (9 oz/2 cups) plain
(all-purpose) flour

1 tablespoon baking powder

2 tablespoons icing
(confectioners') sugar

pinch cayenne pepper

1 teaspoon dry mustard

90 g (3¼ oz/¾ cup) grated strong
cheddar cheese

185 ml (6 fl oz/¾ cup) milk

1 egg

60 ml (2 fl oz/¼ cup) oil

50 g (1¾ oz/⅓ cup) grated cheddar
cheese, extra

1 Preheat the oven to 200°C (400°F/Gas 6). Grease 6 large muffin holes. Place the bacon in a frying pan and cook, stirring, over medium heat for 3–5 minutes, or until golden. Drain on paper towels. Transfer to a small bowl and mix with the chopped egg.

2 Sift the flour and baking powder into a bowl and stir in the sugar, cayenne pepper, mustard, cheddar cheese and ½ teaspoon salt. Make a well in the centre.

3 Place the milk, egg and oil in a bowl, whisk together and pour into the well. Fold gently until combined — the batter should be lumpy.

4 Fill each muffin hole one-third full with the mixture, forming a slight indentation in the centre of each. Divide the egg and bacon filling among the tins, keeping it piled in the middle. Top with the remaining batter.

5 Sprinkle the extra cheddar cheese over the top, then bake for 20–25 minutes, or until the muffins are risen and golden. Cool in the tin for 5 minutes, then transfer to a wire rack to cool completely.

ORANGE POPPY SEED MUFFINS

215 g (7½ oz/1¾ cups) self-raising flour

1 tablespoon caster (superfine) sugar

1 teaspoon baking powder

¼ teaspoon bicarbonate of soda
(baking soda)

1 tablespoon poppy seeds

90 g (3¼ oz) butter

160 g (5½ oz/½ cup) orange marmalade

1 egg, lightly beaten

185 ml (6 fl oz/¾ cup) milk

icing (confectioners') sugar, to dust

1   Preheat the oven to 210°C (415°F/Gas 6–7). Lightly grease a 12-hole standard muffin tin. Sift flour, sugar, baking powder and soda into a mixing bowl. Add the poppy seeds and stir. Make a well in the centre.

2   Combine the butter and marmalade in a small saucepan and stir over a low heat until marmalade becomes runny and the butter has melted. Add the butter mixture and combined egg and milk to flour mixture, stir until just combined. Do not overmix, the batter should be quite lumpy.

3   Spoon the batter evenly into the muffin holes and cook for 10–12 minutes or until golden. Loosen the muffins with a flat-bladed knife and transfer to a wire rack. Dust with the icing sugar.

Note: For a delicious topping, beat 60 g (2 oz) soft butter, 2 tablespoons icing sugar and 1 teaspoon orange rind until light and creamy. Cut a small section from the top of the muffin, fill with mixture and replace the tops.

OLIVE AND THYME MUFFINS

MAKES 12

375 g (13 oz/3 cups) self-raising flour

35 g (1¼ oz/⅓ cup) grated
parmesan cheese

140 g (5 oz/¾ cup) mixed black and
green olives, chopped

3 tablespoons fresh thyme leaves

375 ml (13 fl oz/1½ cups) milk

2 eggs

60 ml (2 fl oz/¼ cup) olive oil

12 sprigs fresh thyme, to garnish
(optional)

1 **Preheat the oven** to 180°C (350°F/Gas 4). Grease a 12-hole standard muffin tin. Sift the flour and ½ teaspoon salt into a bowl. Add the cheese, olives and thyme and stir together. Make a well in the centre.

2 **Lightly whisk together** the milk, eggs and oil in a bowl and pour into the well. Fold gently until just combined — the batter should be lumpy.

3 **Divide mixture** evenly among the muffin holes. Place a thyme sprig on top of each muffin for garnish. Bake for 20 minutes, or until muffins come away from the side of the tin. Cool for 5 minutes, then transfer to a wire rack to cool completely.

OAT AND GOLDEN SYRUP MUFFINS

MAKES 12

TOPPING

50 g (1¾ oz/½ cup) oats

80 g (2¾ oz/⅓ cup) firmly packed soft brown sugar

30 g (1 oz/⅓ cup) desiccated coconut

40 g (1½ oz) unsalted butter, chopped

310 g (11 oz/2½ cups) self-raising flour

2 teaspoons baking powder

115 g (4 oz/½ cup) firmly packed soft brown sugar

250 ml (9 fl oz/1 cup) buttermilk

2 eggs, lightly beaten

2 teaspoons natural vanilla extract

100 g (3½ oz) unsalted butter, chopped

115 g (4 oz/⅓ cup) golden syrup (dark corn syrup)

1 Preheat the oven to 200°C (400°F/Gas 6). Lightly grease a 12-hole standard muffin tin. To make the topping, place the oats, sugar and coconut in a bowl and combine. Add the butter and rub it in with your fingertips until crumbly.

2 Sift the flour and baking powder into a bowl and stir in the sugar. Make a well in the centre.

3 Whisk the buttermilk, eggs and vanilla in a bowl until combined and pour into the well.

4 Melt the butter and golden syrup in a small saucepan over low heat. Pour into the well. Fold mixture gently until just combined — the batter should be lumpy.

5 Divide the mixture among the muffin holes, then sprinkle on the topping. Bake for 20–25 minutes, or until the muffins come away from the side of the tin. Cool briefly, then transfer to a wire rack.

PUMPKIN AND WALNUT MUFFINS

MAKES 12

375 g (13 oz/2½ cups) pumpkin, peeled and roughly chopped

310 g (11 oz/2½ cups) self-raising flour

2 teaspoons mixed (pumpkin pie) spice

60 g (2½ oz/½ cup) chopped walnuts

165 g (5¾ oz/¾ cup) firmly packed soft brown sugar

250 ml (9 fl oz/1 cup) buttermilk

2 eggs

90 g (3¼ oz) unsalted butter, melted and cooled

90 g (3¼ oz/¾ cup) icing (confectioners') sugar

80 ml (2½ fl oz/⅓ cup) maple syrup

1 tablespoon chopped walnuts, extra

1   Preheat the oven to 200°C (400°F/Gas 6). Line a 12-hole standard muffin tin with muffin papers. Steam the chopped pumpkin for 10 minutes, or until tender. Mash well and set aside until it has cooled.

2   Sift the flour and mixed spice into a large bowl and stir in the walnuts and brown sugar. Make a well in the centre.

3   Place the buttermilk, eggs and butter in a bowl, whisk together and pour into the well. Fold mixture gently until just combined — the batter should be lumpy. Fold in the pumpkin.

4   Divide the mixture evenly among the muffin holes. Bake for 20 minutes, or until golden. Cool for 5 minutes, then transfer to a wire rack to cool a little.

5   Meanwhile, to make the icing (frosting), put icing sugar and maple syrup in a small bowl and stir until a brushable paste forms. Brush icing all over the warm muffins, sprinkle with the extra walnuts, then cool. The icing will set as the muffins cool.

HOT CROSS MUFFINS

MAKES 12

250 g (9 oz/2 cups) self-raising flour

3 teaspoons ground cinnamon

125 g (4½ oz) unsalted butter, chopped

160 g (5½ oz/1 cup) sultanas (golden raisins)

45 g (1½ oz/¼ cup) mixed peel

185 g (6½ oz/¾ cup) caster (superfine) sugar

185 ml (6 fl oz/¾ cup) milk

2 eggs, lightly beaten

2 teaspoons powdered gelatine

2 tablespoons caster (superfine) sugar, extra

60 g (2¼ oz/½ cup) icing (confectioners') sugar

2 teaspoons lemon juice

1 **Preheat the oven** to 200°C (400°F/Gas 6). Grease a 12-hole standard muffin tin. Sift the flour and cinnamon into a large bowl, add the butter and rub it in with your fingertips until the mixture resembles fine breadcrumbs. Stir in the sultanas, peel and caster sugar. Make a well in the centre.

2 **Place the milk and eggs** in a bowl, whisk and pour into the well. Fold gently until just combined — the batter should be lumpy.

3 **Divide among the muffin holes.** Bake for 20–25 minutes, or until the muffins come away from the side of the tin. Cool briefly, then transfer to a wire rack.

4 **Meanwhile,** to make the glaze, combine the gelatine, extra sugar and 2 tablespoons water in a small saucepan and stir over low heat for 1 minute, or until the sugar and gelatine are dissolved, then remove from the heat. Brush warm muffins with the glaze a couple of times, then cool.

5 **To make the icing (frosting),** mix the icing sugar and lemon juice until smooth. Spoon the icing into the corner of a small plastic bag, snip off the end and pipe a cross on each muffin and allow to set.

PEANUT BUTTER AND SOUR CREAM MUFFINS

MAKES 6

12 sugar cubes

80 g (2¾ oz/½ cup) roughly chopped roasted unsalted peanuts

280 g (10 oz/2¼ cups) self-raising flour

125 g (4½ oz/½ cup) caster (superfine) sugar

125 g (4½ oz/½ cup) crunchy peanut butter

185 g (6½ oz/¾ cup) sour cream

185 ml (6 fl oz/¾ cup) milk

2 eggs

90 g (3¼ oz) unsalted butter, melted and cooled

160 g (5½ oz/⅔ cup) sour cream, extra

1   **Preheat the oven** to 200°C (400°F/Gas 6). Grease 6 large muffin holes.

2   **Lightly crush the sugar cubes** in a plastic bag into medium-sized pieces, then put in a small bowl. Add the peanuts and stir.

3   **Sift the flour** into a bowl and stir in the caster sugar. Make a well in the centre.

4   **Place the peanut butter,** sour cream, milk, eggs and butter in a bowl, combine and pour into the well. Fold gently until just combined — the batter should be lumpy.

5   **Divide half the batter** among the muffin holes. Top each with 1 heaped tablespoon of the extra sour cream and spoon the remaining batter evenly over the top, then sprinkle with the peanut mixture.

6   **Bake the muffins** for 20–25 minutes, or until golden. Cool for 5 minutes, then transfer to a wire rack.

BANANA MUFFINS WITH CARAMEL SYRUP

MAKES 12

250 g (9 oz/2 cups) self-raising flour

125 g (4½ oz/½ cup) caster (superfine) sugar

250 ml (9 fl oz/1 cup) milk

1 egg

2 teaspoons natural vanilla extract

75 g (2½ oz) unsalted butter, melted and cooled

240 g (8½ oz/1 cup) mashed banana

300 g (10½ oz) sugar

1 Preheat the oven to 200°C (400°F/Gas 6). Grease 12 standard muffin holes.

2 Sift the flour into a bowl and stir in the caster sugar. Make a well in the centre.

3 Put the milk, egg and vanilla in a bowl. Whisk and pour into the well. Add the butter and banana and fold until just combined — the batter should be lumpy.

4 Divide among the muffin holes. Bake for about 20-25 minutes, or until lightly golden.

5 To make the syrup, put the sugar and about 100 ml (3 fl oz) of water in a small saucepan over medium heat and stir until the sugar dissolves. Increase the heat and cook for 8 minutes, or until golden. Remove from the heat and add 4 tablespoons of water (be careful — it will spit). Stir until the caramel is smooth.

6 Allow the muffins to cool in the tin for 5 minutes, then transfer them to a wire rack to cool completely. Drizzle with the syrup.

STRAWBERRY AND PASSIONFRUIT MUFFINS

MAKES 12

215 g (7½ oz/1¾ cup) self-raising flour

pinch salt

1 teaspoon baking powder

½ teaspoon bicarbonate of soda

60 g (2¼ oz/¼ cup) caster (superfine) sugar

175 g (6 oz/1 cup) fresh strawberries, chopped

125 g (4½ oz/½ cup) passionfruit pulp, tinned or fresh

1 egg

185 ml (6½ fl oz/¾ cup) milk

60 g (2¼ oz) unsalted butter, melted

whipped cream, to serve

fresh strawberries, halved, extra

icing (confectioners') sugar, to dust

1 **Preheat the oven** to 210°C (415°F/Gas 6–7). Lightly grease a 12-hole standard muffin tin.

2 **Sift the flour,** salt, baking powder, soda and sugar into a mixing bowl. Add the strawberries and stir to combine. Make a well in the centre.

3 **Place the egg** and milk in a separate mixing bowl and stir to combine. Add the passionfruit pulp and egg mixture to the flour mixture. Pour the melted butter all at once and lightly stir with a fork until just combined. Do not overmix, the batter should look quite lumpy.

4 **Spoon the mixture** into prepared tin and bake for about 12–15 minutes, or until golden brown. Loosen muffins with a flat-bladed knife and turn out onto a wire rack to cool. Top with whipped cream and fresh strawberry halves and sprinkle with icing sugar, if desired.

Note: Folding the fruit through the dry mixture helps it to be evenly distributed throughout.

APPLE, BUTTERMILK, MAPLE SYRUP AND BRAN MUFFINS

MAKES 12

70 g (2½ oz/1 cup) unprocessed bran

375 ml (13 fl oz/1½ cups) buttermilk

185 ml (6 fl oz/¾ cup) maple syrup

1 egg, lightly beaten

60 ml (2 fl oz/¼ cup) vegetable oil

1 cooking apple (such as granny smith), peeled, cored and chopped

70 g (2½ oz/½ cup) hazelnuts, toasted, peeled (see tip, below) and chopped

250 g (9 oz/2 cups) self-raising flour

1 teaspoon ground cinnamon

1 **Preheat the oven** to 180°C (350°F/Gas 4). Grease a 12-hole standard muffin tin, or line the holes with paper cases.

2 **Combine the bran** and buttermilk in a bowl, stirring to mix well, then set aside for 5 minutes. Add the maple syrup, egg, oil, apple and hazelnuts and stir to combine well. Sift flour and cinnamon over the mixture, then gently fold in until just combined. Do not overmix — the batter will still be lumpy.

3 **Divide the mixture** evenly among the muffin holes. Bake for 20–25 minutes, or until golden and a skewer inserted in the centre of a muffin comes out clean. Cool in the tin for 2 minutes before transferring to a wire rack.

Note: To toast the hazelnuts, put them in a single layer on a large baking tray. Toast either in the oven at 180°C (350°F/Gas 4) or under a preheated grill (broiler) for about 2 minutes (turn them after 1 minute and watch carefully, as nuts burn quickly). Tip into a tea towel (dish towel) and rub the skins off. Not all the skins will come off entirely — don't worry about those that don't.

APPLE AND CINNAMON MUFFINS

MAKES 12

300 g (10½ oz/2 cups) self-raising flour

140 g (5 oz/¾ cup, lightly packed) soft
brown sugar

1 teaspoon cinnamon

160 ml (5¼ fl oz/⅔ cup) milk

4 tablespoons canola oil

2 eggs, whisked

2 ripe apples, peeled, grated

1 Preheat the oven to 180°C (350°F/Gas 4). Lightly grease 12 large muffin holes.

2 Sift the flour, sugar and cinnamon into a large bowl. In a separate bowl, combine the milk, oil and eggs. Add the milk mixture and apples to the flour mixture. Mix until just combined. Spoon evenly among the muffin holes.

3 Bake for 18–20 minutes, or until lightly golden. Leave for 5 minutes, then turn out onto a wire rack to cool.

ALMOND, BERRY AND YOGHURT MUFFINS

MAKES 12

185g (6½ oz/1½ cups) plain (all-purpose) flour

3 teaspoons baking powder

115 g (4 oz/1 cup) ground almonds

185g (6½ oz/¾ cup) caster (superfine) sugar

2 eggs

125 g (4½ oz) unsalted butter, melted, cooled

250 g (9 oz/1 cup) plain (all-purpose) yoghurt

300 g (10½ oz) blueberries or raspberries

2 tablespoons flaked almonds

1 **Preheat the oven** to 180°C (350°F/Gas 4). Grease 12 standard muffin holes.

2 **Sift the flour** and baking powder into a large bowl and stir in the ground almonds and sugar. Make a well in the centre.

3 **Put the eggs,** butter and yoghurt in a bowl, whisk and pour into the well. Fold gently until well combined — the batter should be lumpy.

4 **Fold in the berries.** Divide the mixture among the muffin holes. Top each muffin with flaked almonds.

5 **Bake** for 20 minutes, or until lightly golden. Cool for 5 minutes, then transfer to a wire rack.

POLENTA, SEMI-DRIED TOMATO, PECORINO AND BASIL MUFFINS

**MAKES 12 MUFFINS OR
48 MINI MUFFINS**

155 g (5½ oz/1¼ cups) self-raising flour

110 g (3¾ oz/¾ cup) polenta

60 g (2¼ oz/¾ cup) grated
pecorino cheese

1 egg, lightly beaten

250 ml (9 fl oz/1 cup) milk

80 ml (2½ fl oz/⅓ cup) olive oil

40 g (1½ oz/¼ cup) chopped semi-dried
(sun-blushed) tomatoes

15 g (½ oz/¼ cup) chopped basil

1 **Preheat the oven** to 180°C (350°F/Gas 4). Grease a 12-hole standard muffin tin or two 24-hole mini muffin tins, or line the holes with paper cases.

2 **Sift the flour** into a large bowl, then stir in the polenta and pecorino and season with freshly ground black pepper. Make a well in the centre. Combine the egg, milk and oil in a bowl, then pour into the well. Add the tomatoes and basil and stir quickly until just combined. Do not overmix — the batter will still be slightly lumpy.

3 **Divide the mixture** evenly between the muffin holes. Bake for 20–25 minutes (or 10–12 minutes for mini muffins), or until the muffins are golden and come away from the sides of the tin. Cool in the tin for 2 minutes before transferring to a wire rack. Serve warm.

Note: Most muffins should be left to cool for a few minutes in the tins once out of the oven. Don't leave them for too long or trapped steam will make the bases soggy.

COFFEE PECAN STRUDEL MUFFINS

MAKES 9

215 g (7 oz/1¾ cups) self-raising flour

1 teaspoon baking powder

60 g (2 oz/¼ cup) caster (superfine) sugar

60 g (2 oz/½ cup) finely chopped pecans

1 tablespoon instant coffee powder

1 tablespoon boiling water

1 egg

185 ml (6 fl oz/¾ cup) milk

80 ml (2¾ fl oz/⅓ cup) peanut or safflower oil

icing (confectioners') sugar, to dust

STREUSEL TOPPING

30 g (1 oz/¼ cup) self-raising flour

30 g (1 oz) butter

2 tablespoons soft brown sugar

1 teaspoon cinnamon

2 tablespoons finely chopped pecans

1 **Preheat the oven** to 210°C (415°F/Gas 6–7). Lightly grease nine holes of a 12-hole muffin tin. Sift the flour and baking powder into a mixing bowl. Add the caster sugar and pecans. Make a well in the centre.

2 **Combine the coffee powder** with boiling water and stir until dissolved. Cool and add to the flour mixture. In a separate bowl, combine the egg, milk and oil. Add to flour mixture and stir until just combined. Do not overmix — the batter should look quite lumpy.

3 **To make the topping,** place the flour into a mixing bowl. Rub the butter into the flour until the mixture resembles coarse breadcrumbs. Add the sugar, cinnamon and pecans and mix until well combined.

4 **Spoon the muffin mixture** into the prepared tin. Sprinkle with the topping and bake for 10–12 minutes, or until golden brown. Loosen the muffins with a flat-bladed knife and turn out onto a wire rack to cool completely. Sprinkle with icing sugar, if desired.

WHITE CHOC-CHIP AND CREAM CHEESE MU

MAKES 12

125 g (4½ oz) unsalted butter, softened

185 g (6½ oz/¾ cup) caster (superfine) sugar

2 eggs, lightly beaten

1 teaspoon natural vanilla extract

250 g (9 oz/2 cups) self-raising flour, sifted

125 ml (4 fl oz/½ cup) buttermilk

280 g (10 oz/1⅔ cups) white chocolate bits (chocolate chips)

white chocolate, shaved, to decorate

CREAM CHEESE ICING (FROSTING)

100 g (3½ oz) white chocolate

60 ml (2 fl oz/¼ cup) cream

200 g (7 oz/¾ cup) cream cheese, softened

40 g (1½ oz/⅓ cup) icing (confectioners') sugar

1 Preheat the oven to 170°C (325°F/Gas 3). Lightly grease a 12-hole standard muffin tin.

2 Beat the butter and sugar in a large bowl with electric beaters until pale and creamy. Gradually add the egg, beating well after each addition. Add the vanilla extract and beat until combined. Fold in the flour alternately with the buttermilk, then fold in the chocolate bits.

3 Fill each muffin hole three-quarters full with the mixture and bake for 20 minutes, or until a skewer comes out clean when inserted in the centre of each cake. Leave in the tins for 5 minutes before turning out onto a wire rack to cool. Loosen around the edges if the cakes stick to the tins.

4 To make the icing (frosting), melt the chocolate and cream in a small saucepan over low heat until smooth. Cool slightly, then add to the cream cheese and icing sugar and beat until smooth. Spread the icing over cakes and garnish with white chocolate shavings

SPICY VEGETABLE MUFFINS

MAKES 12

250 g (9 oz/2 cups) self-raising flour

3 teaspoons curry powder

80 g (2¾ oz/½ cup) grated carrot

60 g (2¼ oz/½ cup) grated
orange sweet potato

125 g (4½ oz/1 cup) grated
cheddar cheese

90 g (3¼ oz) butter, melted

1 egg, lightly beaten

185 ml (6 fl oz/¾ cup) milk

1 Preheat the oven to 180°C (350°F/Gas 4). Lightly grease a 12-hole standard muffin tin, or line the muffin tin with paper cases. Sift the flour, curry powder and some salt and pepper into a bowl. Add the carrot, sweet potato and cheese and mix through with your fingertips until the ingredients are evenly combined. Make a well in the centre.

2 Combine the butter, egg and milk and add to the flour mixture all at once. Using a wooden spoon, stir until the ingredients are just combined. Don't overmix — the batter will still be slightly lumpy.

3 Divide the mixture evenly among the holes — fill each hole to about three-quarters full. Bake for 20–25 minutes, or until golden and a skewer inserted into the centre of a muffin comes out clean. Leave in the tin for a couple of minutes. Gently loosen each muffin with a flat-bladed knife before turning out onto a wire rack. Serve warm or at room temperature.

CHOCOLATE HAZELNUT MUFFINS

MAKES 12

200 g (7 oz/1½ cups) hazelnuts

185 g (6½ oz/6¼ oz) unsalted butter

6 egg whites

155 g (5½ oz/1¼ cups) plain (all-purpose) flour

30 g (1 oz/¼ cup) cocoa powder

250 g (9 oz/2 cups) icing (confectioners') sugar

icing (confectioners') sugar, extra, to dust

1   **Preheat the oven** to 200°C (400°F/Gas 6). Lightly grease 12 standard friand tins or a standard muffin tin. Spread the hazelnuts out on a baking tray and bake for 8–10 minutes, or until fragrant (take care not to burn). Put in a clean tea towel (dish towel) and rub vigorously to loosen the skins. Discard the skins. Cool. Process in a food processor until finely ground.

2   **Place the butter** in a small pan and melt over medium heat, then cook for 3–4 minutes, or until it turns a deep golden colour. Strain any dark solids and set aside to cool (the colour will become deeper on standing).

3   **Lightly whisk the egg** whites in a bowl until frothy but not firm. Sift the flour, cocoa powder and icing sugar into a large bowl and stir in the ground hazelnuts. Make a well in the centre, add the egg whites and butter and mix until combined.

4   **Spoon mixture** into the friand holes until three-quarters filled. Bake for 20–25 minutes, or until a skewer inserted into the centre comes out clean. Leave in the tin for a few minutes, then cool on a wire rack. Dust with icing sugar, to serve.

LOW-FAT APRICOT AND ORANGE MUFFINS

MAKES 12

140 g (5 oz/¾ cup) dried apricots, roughly chopped

grated zest from 1 orange

125 ml (4 fl oz/½ cup) freshly squeezed orange juice

250 g (9 oz/2 cups) self-raising flour

175 g (6 oz/½ cup) honey

30 g (1 oz) unsalted butter, melted

185 ml (6 fl oz/¾ cup) skim milk

1 egg, lightly beaten

1 Preheat the oven to 180°C (350°F/Gas 4). Grease a 12-hole standard muffin tin, or line the holes with paper cases.

2 Combine the apricots, orange zest and juice in a small saucepan and cook over medium heat until just warmed through. Remove from the heat and cool.

3 Sift the flour into a large bowl and make a well in the centre. Combine the honey, butter, milk and egg in a bowl, stirring to mix well. Pour into the well, then add the apricot mixture and stir quickly until just combined. Do not overmix — the batter will still be slightly lumpy.

4 Divide the mixture evenly between the muffin holes. Bake for 20–25 minutes, or until golden and a skewer inserted into the centre of a muffin comes out clean. Cool in the tin for 2 minutes before transferring to a wire rack.

Note: When making muffins, always sift the flour. This will aerate the flour and ensure a light muffin.

STRAWBERRY CHEESECAKE MUFFINS

MAKES 6

250 g (9 oz/1⅔ cups) strawberries, hulled

125 g (4½ oz/½ cup) caster (superfine) sugar

85 g (3 oz/⅓ cup) cream cheese

1 tablespoon strawberry liqueur

175 g (6 oz/1⅓ cups) plain (all-purpose) flour

1 tablespoon baking powder

1 tablespoon butter, melted

1 teaspoon finely grated orange zest

1 egg

125 ml (4 fl oz/½ cup) milk

icing (confectioners') sugar, to dust

1 Preheat the oven to 180°C (350°F/Gas 4). Lightly grease six 125 ml (½ cup) non-stick muffin holes with oil. Set aside six small strawberries.

2 Place half the sugar in a bowl with the cream cheese and combine well. Place the remaining strawberries in a blender or food processor with the strawberry liqueur and remaining sugar, and blend until smooth. Strain through a fine sieve to remove the strawberry seeds.

3 Sift the flour and baking powder together in a large bowl and stir in the butter, orange zest and ½ teaspoon salt. In a separate bowl, beat the egg and milk together, then add to the dry ingredients and mix well until combined. Do not overmix.

4 Spoon half of the mixture into the base of the muffin holes, then add a strawberry and a teaspoon of the cheese mixture. Top with the remaining muffin mixture and bake for 15 minutes, or until cooked and golden. Remove from the tins and cool slightly. Place a muffin on each serving plate, dust with icing sugar and serve drizzled with the sauce.

BABY COFFEE AND WALNUT SOUR CREAM MUFFINS

MAKES 24

75 g (2½ oz) walnuts

155 g (5½ oz/⅔ cup) firmly packed soft brown sugar

125 g (4½ oz) unsalted butter, softened

2 eggs, lightly beaten

125 g (4½ oz/1 cup) self-raising flour

80 g (2¾ oz/⅓ cup) sour cream

1 tablespoon coffee and chicory essence or strong black coffee

1 **Preheat the oven** to 160°C (315°F/Gas 2–3). Lightly grease two 12-hole 30 ml (1 fl oz) baby muffin tins.

2 **Process the walnuts** and 45 g (1½ oz/¼ cup) of the brown sugar in a food processor until the walnuts are roughly chopped into small pieces. Transfer to a mixing bowl.

3 **Cream the butter** and remaining sugar together in the food processor until pale and creamy. With the motor running, gradually add the egg and process until smooth. Add the flour and blend until well mixed. Add the sour cream and essence and process until thoroughly mixed.

4 **Spoon ½ teaspoon** of the walnut and sugar mixture into the base of each muffin hole, followed by a heaped teaspoon of the cake mixture. Sprinkle a little more walnut mixture over the top, add another heaped teaspoon of the cake mixture and top with the remaining walnut mixture.

5 **Bake for 20 minutes,** or until risen and springy to the touch. Leave in the tins for 5 minutes. Remove the cakes using a flat-bladed knife to loosen the side and base, then transfer to a wire rack to cool completely.

SCONES

PLAIN SCONES

MAKES 12

250 g (9 oz/2 cups) self-raising flour

pinch salt, optional (see Note)

30 g (1 oz) unsalted butter, cut into
  small pieces

125 ml (4 fl oz/½ cup) milk

80 ml (2½ fl oz/⅓ cup) water

milk, extra, to glaze

jam and whipped cream, to serve

1   Preheat the oven to 210°C (415°F/Gas 6–7). Lightly grease a baking tray. Sift the flour and salt, if using, into a large mixing bowl. Add the butter and rub in lightly using your fingertips.

2   Make a well in the centre of the flour. Add almost all of the combined milk and water. Mix with a flat-bladed knife to a soft dough, adding more liquid if necessary.

3   Turn the dough onto a lightly floured surface (use self-raising flour). Knead the dough briefly and lightly until smooth. Press or roll out the dough to form a round about 1–2 cm (½–¾ inch) thick.

4   Cut the dough into rounds using a floured round 5 cm (2 inch) cutter. Place the rounds on the prepared tray and glaze with the milk. Bake for 10–12 minutes, or until golden brown. Serve with jam and whipped cream.

Note: Add a pinch of salt to your scones, even sweet ones. Salt acts as a flavour enhancer and will not be tasted in the cooked product.

SULTANA SCONES

MAKES 12

250 g (8 oz/2 cups) self-raising flour

pinch salt

30 g (1 oz) butter, cut into small pieces

90 g (3¼ oz/⅓ cup) caster (superfine) sugar

30 g (1 oz/¼ cup) sultanas (golden raisins)

1 egg, lightly beaten

185 ml (6 fl oz/¾ cup) milk

extra milk, to glaze

butter, to serve

1 Preheat the oven to 210°C (415°F/Gas 6–7). Lightly grease a baking tray. Sift the flour and salt into a large mixing bowl. Add the butter and rub in lightly with fingertips.

2 Add the sugar and sultanas and stir to combine. Make a well in the centre of the mixture. Add the egg and almost all the milk. Mix quickly, with a flat-bladed knife, to a soft dough, adding more milk if necessary. Turn out onto a lightly floured surface and knead briefly until smooth. Press or roll out to form a round about 2 cm (¾ inch) thick.

3 Cut the dough into rounds using a floured plain 5 cm (2 inch) cutter or cut into squares using a floured knife. Place the rounds close together on the prepared tray and brush with extra milk.

4 Bake for 10–12 minutes, or until golden brown. Serve with butter.

WHOLEMEAL APPLE SCONES

MAKES 12

150 g (5 oz/1 cup) wholemeal self-
  raising flour

125 g (4 oz/1 cup) self-raising flour

pinch salt

1½ teaspoons cinnamon

45 g (1½ oz/¼ cup) soft brown sugar

1 green apple, peeled and grated

30 g (1 oz) butter, melted

125 ml (4 fl oz/½ cup) skim milk

milk, extra, for glazing

1 tablespoon caster sugar, for sprinkling

1 Preheat oven to 210°C (415°F/Gas 6–7). Brush oven tray with melted butter or oil. Sift the flours, salt and 1 teaspoon of cinnamon into a large bowl, returning the husks. Add the sugar and apple and stir until combined.

2 Make a well in the centre of the flour mixture. Add the butter and almost all of the milk. Mix quickly with a flat-bladed knife to form a smooth dough, adding more milk, if necessary.

3 Knead the dough briefly on a lightly floured surface until smooth. Pat into a 20 cm (8 inch) round and place on the prepared tray.

4 Score the dough into 8 even wedges, cutting almost all the way through. Brush with the extra milk and sprinkle with the caster sugar and remaining cinnamon. Bake for 20–25 minutes or until golden brown. Slice into 8 portions when cool and serve with butter.

Note: The size and moisture content of the apple will dictate how much milk is needed to form a soft dough. Add the extra milk in very small amounts and try not to overwork the dough.

RASPBERRY BUN SCONES

MAKES 8

250 g (8 oz/2 cups) self-raising flour

pinch salt

2 tablespoons caster (superfine) sugar

125 ml (4 fl oz/½ cup) milk

30 g (1 oz) butter, melted

80 ml (2¼ fl oz/⅓ cup) water

1 tablespoon raspberry jam

1 tablespoon milk, extra

caster (superfine) sugar, extra

butter, to serve

1 Preheat the oven to 210°C (415°F/Gas 6–7). Lightly grease a baking tray. Sift the flour and salt into a large mixing bowl. Add the sugar and stir to combine.

2 Make a well in the centre of the flour. Place milk and melted butter in a separate bowl and combine. Add to the flour mixture all at once, reserving a teaspoonful for glazing. Add almost all of the water. Mix quickly, using a flat-bladed knife, to form a soft dough, adding more water if necessary.

3 Knead dough briefly on a lightly floured surface until smooth. Cut the dough into 8 rounds using a floured 7 cm (2¾ inch) cutter. Turn each scone over and make an small indentation in the centre with your thumb. Place ½ teaspoon of jam in the indentation and fold over dough. Place rounds, well apart, on the prepared tray and flatten tops. Brush with the milk and sprinkle with the extra caster sugar.

4 Bake for 10–12 minutes, or until golden. Serve warm with butter.

POTATO AND OLIVE SCONES

MAKES 15

250 g (8 oz) potatoes, peeled and chopped

125 ml (4 fl oz/½ cup) milk

pepper, to taste

250 g (9 oz/2 cups) self-raising flour

30 g (1 oz) butter

60 g (2 oz/¼ cup) black olives, seeded and chopped

3–4 teaspoons chopped rosemary

125 ml (4 fl oz/½ cup) water

milk, extra, for glazing

1 Preheat the oven to 210°C (415°F/Gas 6–7). Brush an oven tray with melted butter or oil. Boil or microwave the potatoes until tender. Mash the potatoes with the milk and season with freshly ground black pepper.

2 Sift the flour into a large bowl and add the butter, rubbing in using your fingertips. Add the olives and rosemary and stir until just combined.

3 Make a well in the centre and add the mashed potato and almost all of the water. Mix with a flat-bladed knife to a soft dough, adding more liquid if necessary.

4 Knead the dough briefly on a lightly floured surface until smooth. Press out the dough to 2 cm thickness. Using a floured 5 cm plain round cutter, cut rounds from the dough and place on the prepared tray. Brush with extra milk and cook for 10–15 minutes until golden brown.

5 Serve the scones hot or cold with butter.

Note: The saltiness of the olives means that no extra salt needs to be added to the dough.

CHEESE PINWHEEL SCONES

MAKES 10

250 g (9 oz/2 cups) plain (all-purpose) flour

1 tablespoon baking powder

pinch of cayenne pepper

30g (1 oz) unsalted butter, chilled and diced

185 ml (6 fl oz/¾ cup) milk

FILLING

40 g (1½ oz/¼ cup) goat's cheese, crumbled

40 g (1½ oz/½ cup) grated parmesan cheese

40 g (1½ oz/⅓ cup) grated mature cheddar cheese

2 tablespoons chopped flat-leaf (Italian) parsley

1 Preheat the oven to 220°C (425°F/Gas 7). Grease or line a baking tray.

2 Sift the flour, baking powder, a pinch of salt and cayenne into a large mixing bowl. Using your fingertips, rub in butter until the mixture resembles breadcrumbs, Add the milk and, using a flat-bladed knife, mix to form a soft dough, Add a little extra flour if the dough is too sticky,

3 Turn the dough out onto a floured work surface and roll out to form a 20 x 25 cm (8 x 10 inch) rectangle. Sprinkle the goat's cheese over the surface, then sprinkle over the parmesan, cheddar and parsley, Starting from the long side, roll the dough into a cylinder. Cut the cylinder into 10 equal 2 cm (¾ inch) thick slices, Transfer the slices to a baking tray, spacing them 2 cm (¾ inch) apart,

4 Bake for 10–12 minutes, until golden and cooked through, Cool on a wire rack. Serve warm.

PUMPKIN AND SAGE SCONES

MAKES 8

250 g (9 oz/2 cups) self-raising flour

250 g (9 oz/1 cup) cooked and puréed
    pumpkin (winter squash)

20 g (¾ oz) cold unsalted butter,
    chopped

1 tablespoon chopped sage

1–2 tablespoons milk

1　**Preheat the oven** to 180°C (350°F/Gas 4). Line a baking tray with baking paper.

2　**Sift the flour** into a bowl with a pinch of sea salt. Using your fingertips, rub the pumpkin and butter into the flour, then stir in the sage.

3　**Bring the mixture** together with a little milk, then turn out onto the baking tray. Shape into a round and roll out to about 3 cm (1¼ inches) thick.

4　**Gently mark** or cut the scone into eight wedges. Bake for 15–20 minutes, or until lightly browned and cooked through. Serve warm.

WHOLEMEAL DATE SCONES

MAKES 16

185 g (6 oz/1½ cups) self-raising flour

225 g (7 oz/1½ cups) wholemeal
self-raising flour

½ teaspoon baking powder

¼ teaspoon salt

60 g (2 oz) butter, cut into small pieces

2 tablespoons caster (superfine) sugar

185 g (6 oz/1 cup) chopped dates

315 ml (10 fl oz/1¼ cups) buttermilk

125 ml (4 fl oz/½ cup) water

buttermilk, extra, to glaze

butter or whipped cream, to serve

1 **Preheat the oven** to 210°C (415°F/Gas 6–7). Lightly grease a baking tray. Sift the flours, baking powder and salt into a large mixing bowl, returning the husks. Add the chopped butter and rub in lightly using your fingertips. Stir in the sugar and the chopped dates.

2 **Make a well** in the centre of the flour mixture. Add the buttermilk and almost all of the water. Mix quickly, using a flat-bladed knife, to form a soft dough, adding more water if necessary. The dough should have lost its stickiness but not become too dry or tough.

3 **Knead dough briefly** on a lightly floured surface until smooth. Press out the dough with floured hands to form a 2 cm (¾ inch) thick square. Cut into 16 smaller squares. Place the squares on the prepared tray, leaving a 2 cm (¾ inch) gap between each scone. Brush with extra buttermilk.

4 **Bake the scones** for 12–15 minutes, or until golden brown. Serve straight from the oven with butter or whipped cream, if desired.

Note: These scones are heavily textured. Returning the flour husks to the mixture will contribute to this texture. However, it is still necessary to sift the flours as this introduces air through the dry ingredients.

CHEESE AND CHIVE SCONES

MAKES 9

250 g (9 oz/2 cups) self-raising flour

pinch salt

30 g (1 oz) butter

30 g (1 oz/½ cup) grated cheddar cheese

2 tablespoons shredded parmesan cheese

2 tablespoons snipped chives

125 ml (4 fl oz/½ cup) milk

125 ml (4 fl oz/½ cup) water

30 g (1 oz/¼ cup) grated cheddar cheese, extra

1   **Preheat the oven** to 210°C (415°F/Gas 6–7). Brush an oven tray with melted butter or oil. Sift the flour and salt into bowl. Rub in butter using your fingertips. Stir in cheeses and chives.

2   **Make a well** in the centre, add the milk and almost all of the water. Mix lightly with a flat-bladed knife to a soft dough, adding more liquid if necessary.

3   **Knead the dough** briefly on a lightly floured surface until smooth. Press out dough to 2 cm thickness. Using a floured 5 cm plain round cutter, cut rounds from dough. Place rounds on prepared tray and sprinkle with extra cheese.

4   **Cook for 12 minutes** or until cheese is golden in colour.

Note: For crusty scones, allow them to cool, uncovered, on a wire rack. For softer scones, wrap them in a tea towel while they are still warm and leave to cool.

SPICY FRUIT AND NUT SCONES

MAKES 12

250 g (9 oz/2 cups) self-raising flour

pinch salt

30 g (1 oz) butter, chopped

1 tablespoon caster sugar

90 g (3 oz/½ cup) chopped dried fruit medley

2 tablespoons finely chopped walnuts

¼ teaspoon mixed spice

¼ teaspoon ground ginger

¼ teaspoon ground cloves

125 ml (4 fl oz/½ cup) milk

60 ml (2 fl oz/¼ cup) water

milk, extra, for glazing

2 teaspoons caster sugar, extra

½ teaspoon cinnamon

1 Preheat the oven to 210°C (415°F/Gas 6–7). Brush an oven tray with melted butter or oil. Sift the flour and salt into a bowl, add butter and rub into the flour. Add the caster sugar, dried fruit, walnuts, mixed spice, ground ginger and ground cloves and stir to combine.

2 Make a well in the centre. Add almost all of the combined milk and water to flour mixture. Mix lightly, with a flat-bladed knife, to form a soft dough, adding more liquid if necessary.

3 Knead the dough briefly on a lightly floured surface until smooth, then press out the dough to 2 cm thickness. Using a floured 5 cm round cutter, cut rounds from the dough. Place the rounds on the prepared tray and brush with extra milk. Combine caster sugar and cinnamon and sprinkle over scones.

4 Cook for 10–12 minutes until golden brown. Serve the scones warm or cold with butter.

BUTTERMILK SCONES

MAKES 12

250 g (8 oz/2 cups) self-raising flour

pinch salt

30 g (1 oz) butter

280 ml (9 fl oz/1 cup) buttermilk (see Note)

apricot or strawberry jam, to serve

whipped cream, to serve

1 **Preheat the oven** to 210°C (415°F/Gas 6–7). Brush an oven tray with melted butter or oil.

2 **Sift the flour** and salt into a large bowl, add the chopped butter. Using your fingertips, rub the butter into the flour. Add almost all of the buttermilk. Mix lightly, with a flat-bladed knife, to a soft dough, adding more liquid if necessary. The dough should have just lost its stickiness, but not be dried or tough.

3 **Knead the dough briefly** on a lightly floured surface until smooth. Press the dough to 1 cm thickness. Cut dough into rounds with a floured 5 cm plain or fluted cutter. Place the rounds close together on the prepared tray.

4 **Bake for 10–12 minutes** or until golden brown. Serve the scones warm with apricot or strawberry jam and lightly whipped cream.

Note: Buttermilk has a slightly sour, tangy taste. Its acid reacts with the self-raising flour, making the dough rise and is, thus, ideal for baking.

MINI ONION AND PARMESAN SCONES

MAKES 24

30 g (1 oz) butter, chopped

1 small onion, finely chopped

250 g (8 oz/2 cups) self-raising flour, sifted

pinch salt

30 g (1 oz/½ cup) finely grated parmesan cheese

125 ml (4 fl oz/½ cup) milk

125 ml (4 fl oz/½ cup) water

cayenne pepper, for sprinkling (optional)

1   Preheat oven to 210°C (415°F/Gas 6–7). Brush an oven tray with melted butter or oil.

2   Melt the butter in a small pan, add the onion and cook, over low heat, 2–3 minutes or until soft. Cool slightly.

3   Combine the flour, salt and parmesan cheese in a bowl. Make a well in the centre, add the onion and almost all the combined milk and water. Mix lightly, with a flat-bladed knife, to a soft dough, adding more liquid if necessary.

4   Knead the dough briefly on a lightly floured surface until smooth and press out to 2 cm thickness. Cut the dough into rounds with a floured 3 cm plain round cutter. Place the rounds on the prepared tray and sprinkle each lightly with cayenne pepper, if using.

5   Bake for 10–12 minutes or until golden brown. Serve the scones warm or cold, with butter.

Note: Be careful not to use too much flour when kneading or a tough, dry dough will result. Use self-raising flour for your hands and the work surface.

CAKE BASICS

Equipment

CAKE TINS: Using the correct size of cake [tin is] an important part in the success of the finished cake. There are many shapes and sizes of tins from which to choose. Metal cake tins give consistently good results. Avoid using shiny or very dark tins and glass bakeware.

CHANGING TIN SIZES: If you wish to substitute one shape of tin for another, measure the volume of the batter and pour the same amount of water into the tin you intend to use. As long as the water comes at least halfway but no higher than two-thirds of the way up the tin, you can use it. Be sure to check the cake before the minimum baking time so you can adjust the baking time, if necessary.

Ingredients

Each ingredient used in cake baking has a specific role.

FLOUR: This forms the structure of the cake. It is not necessary to sift the flour unless specified.

EGGS: These are also essential to the structure of the cake. They bind the other ingredients together and add flavour and colour. We have used large (60 g/2 oz) eggs in all of our recipes. For baking, eggs should be at room temperature.

BUTTER: Butter supplies flavour, texture and aroma. Try to use unsalted butter in your recipes because it gives cakes a much richer, sweeter flavour. Make sure it is at room temperature so it creams correctly. If colder, it will not cream or aerate well. If it is too soft and oily, it will not aerate at all.

BEATING TECHNIQUE: Beat the butter and sugar, scraping the sides of the bowl occasionally.

MARGARINE: This can be substituted for butter in most cakes but will give some difference in flavour. Avoid diet and whipped margarines as these products contain too much water for use in successful baking.

OIL: In carrot and zucchini cakes, oil gives very moist results. Use a good-quality vegetable oil but avoid olive oil because its flavours is too strong.

SUGAR: Adds sweetness, colour and fine grain to cakes. Granulated sugar is commonly used in baking. Caster (superfine) sugar is too fine for general cake making. Brown sugar produces moist, flavoursome results in fruit cakes. Dark brown sugar gives a more intense flavour than light brown sugar.

MILK: Whole milk is the most commonly used liquid in cake baking, although l ow-fat milk works equally well.

Techniques

Cakes are often classified by the method used to make them. In general, they'll fall into one of four categories: creaming, whisking (beating of whole eggs and/or egg whites), quick mixing, and folding. It is important to understand the differences between these methods and to follow the correct procedures for each one.

CREAMING METHOD: This is the most frequently used method in cake baking. It is used for making butter cakes, chocolate cakes, light fruit cakes and many others. The proportion of butter to sugar varies from recipe to recipe. The best results are obtained by beating butter (which is at room temperature) and sugar in a small mixing bowl with electric beaters. If the recipe has a high proportion of butter to sugar, the mixture will become light and fluffy. If the recipe uses a much greater quantity of sugar than butter, the mixture won't be very light or fluffy, so just beat until the ingredients are well mixed.

FOLDING TECHNIQUE: Run the spoon along the underside of the mixture and up in one sweeping motion. Cut through the centre on the next fold.

Scrape the sides of the bowl with a spatula several times during the creaming process to make sure the sugar and butter are well incorporated. This initial creaming process should take several minute... ...eggs or egg yolks are then added. Be sure to beat these lightly before adding i... ...e butter mixture. Add the beaten eggs gradually, beating thoroughly after ea... ...tion.

Vanilla, grated citrus zest and other flavourings are added at this stage. The mixture is then transferred to a large mixing bowl. Add the dry ingredients and liquid alternately (about one-quarter to one-third of each at a time), stirring gently with a large spoon after each addition. Stir until just combined and the mixture is almost smooth. Take care with this final stage, mixing the ingredients together lightly yet evenly. By beating over-enthusiastically, you are very likely to undo previous good work and produce a heavy, coarse-textured cake.

WHISKING METHOD: This is generally used for sponge cakes and light and airy cake rolls. Eggs are the chief ingredient, used whole or separated. Use the freshest eggs and always have them at room temperature. Whole-egg sponge cakes are made by beating whole eggs in a small mixing bowl with electric beaters for 5 minutes or until thick and pale yellow.

WHISKING METHOD: Whisk eggs together until thick and pale yellow.

Sugar is added gradually, about a tablespoon at a time. Beat constantly for about 10 minutes or until the sugar is dissolved and the mixture is pale yellow and glossy. The sifted dry ingredients are then quickly and lightly folded in.

Eggs can also be beaten with sugar in a heatproof bowl over simmering water (Génoise-style) until mixture is pale yellow and thick — hand-held electric beaters should be used. The mixture is then removed from the heat and beaten with electric beaters until almost doubled in volume. Sifted dry ingredients are then gently folded in.

Most sponge cake recipes call for the eggs to be separated and beaten separately. Take care when separating eggs, because just one small particle of egg yolk (or any type of fat) can ruin beating quality. Separate one at a time into a small glass bowl, then transfer to the bowl for beating.

QUICK MIX METHOD: This fast and simple method is gaining popularity. Melt the butter with flavourings such as brown sugar and chocolate and then pour over the sifted dry ingredients. Make a well in the centre of the dry ingredients beforehand. Stir mixture with a wooden spoon until combined. The eggs are then stirred in, taking care not to overmix.

QUICK MIX METHOD: Make a well in the dry ingredients and pour melted butter and sugar into the centre. Whisk until well combined.

THE FOLDING TECHNIQUE: Using a large metal spoon, fold in the dry ingredients, running the spoon along the underside of the mixture and up in one sweeping action that takes the dry ingredients under and over the egg mixture. Cut down through the centre of the bowl on the next fold, rotating the mixing bowl as you fold. Repeat these actions until the mixture is well combined. Work quickly and lightly to ensure even distribution of ingredients and to avoid overmixing. This is particularly important with some muffin recipes where the mixture should remain a little lumpy.

BEATING THE EGG WHITES: Beating egg whites to the correct consistency is a vital stage in cake making. Use a glass or metal mixing bowl that is clean and dry. Use electric beaters to beat the egg whites until firm peaks form — the whites should hold a straight peak when you lift the beaters out. The sugar is then added gradually while beating constantly, and the mixture is beaten until the sugar is completely dissolved. Rub some of the beaten egg white mixture between your fingers to make sure that there aren't any undissolved sugar crystals in it. The mixture should be very glossy and thick and hold in stiff peaks.

BEATING EGG WHITES: Use a clean glass or metal bowl for beating egg whites. Beat until firm peaks form, then add sugar.

The lightly beaten egg yolks are then added and the mixture is transferred to a large mixing bowl. Use a metal spoon to fold in the sifted dry ingredients quickly and lightly.

MUFFIN BASICS

Perfect muffins

Muffins must be one of the most rewarding things to cook. The first step is to assemble all your ingredients and utensils before you start and remember to always make sure the oven is preheated. Preparing the muffin tin for baking is important. Even though most tins have non-stick surfaces, it is still well worth greasing the holes, especially when making sweet muffins, as the sugar can make them very sticky. Always sift the flour into a mixing bowl as it will aerate the flour and ensure your muffins are light. Next, gently fold in the liquid ingredients with a metal spoon until just combined.

Be careful not to over-beat or the muffins will become tough and rubbery. The mixture should still be quite lumpy at this stage. Divide the mixture evenly among the holes using two metal spoons — fill each hole to about three-quarters full. Always try to use the hole size indicated in the recipe as the cooking time changes if you use a different size. The larger the hole, the longer the baking time.

Bake the muffins for about 20 minutes, or until they are risen, golden and come away slightly from the sides of the holes. Test them by pressing lightly with your fingertips, they are cooked if they feel firm and spring back after you touch them. Another test is to insert a skewer into the centre of the muffin—if it comes out clean they are ready.

Most muffins should be left in the tin for a couple of minutes once out of the oven, but don't leave them too long or trapped steam will make the bases soggy. Using a flat-bladed knife, loosen the muffins and transfer to a wire rack to cool completely before serving or storing.

If you like the idea of having freshly baked muffins for breakfast but don't want to start the day making a mess in the kitchen, simply make a muffin mixture, spoon it into the muffin tin and refrigerate it overnight, ready for baking the following day. Uncooked mixture for the plainer muffins such as chocolate or blueberry, or those without fillings, can be frozen in paper-lined muffin tins for up to a month. To cook the muffins, remove them from the freezer and bake in a preheated 200°C (400°F/Gas 6) oven for 25–30 minutes, or until golden and slightly shrunk away from the sides.

Storage

Muffins will freeze very well. Once they have cooled after baking, place in a freezer bag and freeze for up to three months. When required, thaw and wrap in foil before reheating in a 180°C (350°F/Gas 4) oven for about 8 minutes, or until heated through.

What went wrong?

1. PERFECT: The muffin is even with a nicely risen centre and good golden colouring, it has started to come away from the side of the holes. Muffins need to be cooked in a preheated 200°C (400°F/Gas 6) oven so the batter will set and peak correctly.

2. TOO PEAKED: The crust is too coloured and the muffin too peaked. This is caused by over-beating or baking in an oven that is too hot. The result is rubbery muffins with an uneven shape. Be sure all the dry ingredients are evenly distributed by sifting and mixing them before adding them to the wet ingredients.

3. POORLY RISEN: The muffin texture is too heavy and dense. This can be caused by insufficient raising agent or a missing ingredient.

4. OVERFLOWING MIXTURE: It is very important to make sure you use the size of muffin tin suggested in the recipe you are using. Do not fill the muffin holes more than two-thirds full. This leaves room for the batter to rise as it will often rise by half its volume.

5. UNDERCOOKED: The finished muffin is moist in the centre with insufficient peaking. The muffin is not property coloured and didn't shrink away from the tin. The oven was probably not sufficiently preheated or not hot enough, or the been too short.

Perfect scones

Making great scones is not difficult and they get even easier with practice. All scones are made according to the same principles: add wet ingredients to the dry and mix the dough as briefly and lightly as possible. Because the moisture content of flour varies, you may not need all the liquid stated in your recipe. The amount of liquid the flour absorbs can also change according to the room temperature and even the altitude. Although our recipe uses self-raising flour, some people prefer to use plain flour and add more raising agents such as baking powder. Salt is added to enhance the flavour of all scones, even sweet ones.

It's simple to achieve a good batch of high, light and golden scones. Remember that, unlike bread, which requires vigorous kneading, scone dough simply needs quick, light handling.

Before you begin mixing, preheat the oven to 220°C (425°F/Gas 7) and lightly grease the baking tray or line it with baking paper. Sift the dry ingredients into a mixing bowl. Sifting aerates the dry ingredients and helps achieve lighter scones, so many bakers sift the flour twice. Rub in the butter briefly and lightly with your fingertips until the mixture is crumbly and resembles fine breadcrumbs. Make a well in the centre and add the liquid ingredients. Mix with a flat-bladed knife, using a cutting action, until the dough comes together in clumps, rotating the bowl as you work. Use the remaining milk if the mixture seems dry.

Handle the mixture with great care and a very light hand. If you are heavy-handed and mix too much, or knead, your scones will be very tough. The dough should feel slightly wet and sticky. With floured hands, gently gather the dough together, lift onto a lightly floured surface and pat into a smooth ball. Do not knead. Cut the dough as indicated in the recipe and place on the prepared tray. Gather the dough scraps together and, without too much handling, press out again and cut out more scones.

It is important to cook scones at a high temperature, otherwise the raising agents will not work. If you aren't sure they are cooked, break one open. If it is still doughy in the centre, cook for a few more minutes. For soft scones, wrap them in a dry tea towel (dish towel) while hot. For scones with a crisp top, transfer to a wire rack to cool slightly before wrapping.

Storage

As scones generally contain little fat, they dry out quickly so are best eaten soon after baking. However, they will freeze very successfully for up to three months.

What went wrong?

1. PERFECT: The scone is evenly risen, has a soft crust and soft inside texture and is light golden. The dough should not be overworked, but lightly mixed with a flat-bladed knife until combined.

2. POORLY RISEN: If the scone texture feels heavy and dense, the dough may have been either too dry or too wet. Overworking or mixing the dough too much will also result in heavy scones.

3. UNDERCOOKED: The scone is pale, sticky in the centre and has a dense texture. The cooking time was too short or the oven temperature too low. The oven must be 200°C (425°F/Gas 7).

4. OVERCOOKED: The scone has a dark crust and a dry texture. Either the cooking time was too long or the oven temperature was too hot, so always check the temperature and cooking time.

INDEX